MAN IN TRANSITION

...the roles he plays as father, son friend and lover.

Copyright © 1990 by Kenneth F. Byers
All Rights Reserved
Original Edition Printed-November, 1989
2nd Edition Printed-November, 1990
3rd Edition Printed-November, 1991
Russian Translation and Printing-January, 1992

ISBN 0-9619040-3-8
Library of Congress Catalog
Card number 89-084057

Published by

»Journeys Together«

P.O. Box 1254 • La Mesa, CA • 92044

"...I'm 3/4 through your book now, and it is marvelous. It really speaks to my needs today. The self discoveries that it is bringing about has resulted in a lot of 2 word phrases escaping from my mind and lips. And, they're the same 2 words: "Oh shit!"

Ron Harris,
San Diego, CA
10/02/91

Table of Contents

Forward
Introduction   7
  Personal History
  Vietnam
  The Feminine Principle
  Time Line
PART ONE - DEFINING THE PROBLEM
  My Own Struggle   15
  The Father and Son Heritage   18
  The Growth Continuum   23
  Father Hunger   28
  Peace and Security   31
  Belief Systems   37
  Alive at Twenty   39
PART TWO - THE TOOLS
  Tool # 1 -Communication   43
  Tool # 2 - Unconditional Love   49
  Tool # 3 - The Structure of Relationship   59
  Tool # 4 - Risk and Fear   64
  Tool # 5 - Visualizations/Affirmation   73
  Tool # 6 - Resistance   79
  Tool # 7 - Excellence vs. Perfection   82
  Tool # 8 - The Masculine/Feminine Connection   90
  Tool # 9 - Problems vs. Opportunities   94
  Tool # 10 - Defining the Male   98
  Tool # 11 - Looking Within   102
  Tool # 12 - Feeling vs. Thinking   108
  Tool # 13 - Meditation   112
  Tool # 14 - Rites of Passage   117
  Tool # 15 - Role Modeling/Self-Love   122
  Tool # 16 - Passion   127
  Tool # 17 - Non-workable Relationship   130
  Tool # 18 - Forgiveness   136
  Tool # 19 - What Do You Want?   142
  Tool # 20 - Trust   147
  Tool # 21 - The Gifts We Share   152
  Tool # 22 - Surrender   157
Resources   160

*To Brian Shahn and Jamey Scot:
my beautiful, loving teachers*

Men sure are a curious lot. We are at once steel-like and yet incredibly fragile beings. A true anomaly. We will spend thousands of dollars and as much time as it takes to go to seminars on tax shelters, real estate investment or the latest advances in our particular job responsibility. But when it comes to finding out who we are, how we relate to others, or touching our essence in some way, we either turn on the TV or send our women to the workshops and ask them to fill us in on the high points. We readily acknowledge the problems in the world and troubles in our lives, and then talk football.

But things are changing fast. Men are beginning to wake up to the nightmare of the relationships we have created. Waking from a bad dream is the easy part; recreating our reality is the real challenge. The dream is the divorce rate, substance abuse, aimless careers, social and political apathy. The reality is our God-given natural right to a mentally, spiritually and physically healthy life, and a safe and clean planet.

It's about time.

Few relationships have more effect on a man's life than that which he has with his father. Those of us fortunate enough to have the opportunity to re-experience our father-son history with our own sons know that the son may well continue the cycle with his sons. There can be no greater gift to ourselves, our sons and those sons yet unborn than to make each successive relationship more bountiful than the last. As it is our sons who will fight the future wars or make the future peace, it is our responsibility to give them the time, love and security to allow them their own best choices.

There's a man who is my brother,
I just don't know his name.
But I know his home and family
because I know we feel the same.

And it hurts me when he's hungry
and when his children cry,
I too am a father and
that little one is mine.

john denver

FORWARD

It was 1984, spring as I recall. The nineteenth year of my marriage, eighth year of my manufacturing business. Both had survived the trials of time and fortune, each with its scars and medals. My wife was becoming a successful real estate agent, we were moving up rapidly to the good life. The boys, twelve and fourteen, were, well, they were boys. We were on a roll, and although the term "yuppie" had not yet been coined, we were there.

On those days when business was good, I was a success. No doubt in my mind. When things hit the pits, I followed suit. But I didn't worry much because I had all the answers. I was an entrepreneur, master of my own fate, captain of my ship. The pits were simply part of the game, and everyone surely understood that, even if I couldn't take the time to explain it.

The discovery that my beloved first born had a severe drug and alcohol problem hit me like a bag of wet bricks. The reality that he had been pushing since the seventh grade didn't take hold for months. It took several years to begin to really understand what was going on with him in a way that it could be changed, and the work continues in part through this book, my "Male in Transition" workshops and continuing personal growth. I cannot thank him enough for his gift to me. And also the gift of his younger brother, who saw what was going on and learned from another's pain. A rare and wonderful ability.

Trying to figure out what was going on with my son, how it reflected elsewhere in my life and what I could do about it, have been the gifts I have been given. He gave me an opportunity to look at my own life in a way that has opened whole vistas of new experiences for both of us. I became aware that I could not help him until I understood what the real problems were that took him to that place of desperation. I had to look first to myself and my own values, to what he saw that took him to the brink of destruction, and then to the whole meaning of being male. What I discovered was that I had handled society's picture of success, but had no real idea of what being a success as a man was all about. I had confused trillions of megabytes of information about the meaning of maleness in my brain. *The world had developed the picture of who I should be and I bought in!* It is the same picture that almost every man in America has bought into. Now, five years later, I am still the same person I was then, and know that I always will be. I just have a very different perception of what I do, how I do it and how it affects others.

My values are vastly different today, and so are those of my sons. We each still have much to learn and each will make his mistakes, but our decisions will come from a place of understanding about our responsibility for the results. Our communication still suffers, our contacts not always the most pleasant. There is great power in our relationships and that energy takes many forms. I love them passionately, and that passion is reflected in our conflicts as well. It will probably always be so. That's who we are. I have come to discover that it is not important what the world thinks about our relationship, as long as it serves *us* positively, and allows us to grow and explore our potentials. What I have found also is that each lesson learned with my sons has been a life lesson. One that has impacted all areas of my life, personal as well as business. I have learned to listen with my heart.

This is a book about men and relationships. Generally, all relationships, and specifically the father-son relationship. The power that resides in the father-son interaction is just beginning to be understood and talked about as the core relationship of life itself for both men and women. The intention here is to present some ways of looking at the process of how we live our lives, so that both men and women may understand and appreciate the essence and meaning of what being a man in our times is all about. He is a new male in the sense that today's male experience is totally different from any male experience in the history of mankind.

Men's concepts of their own maleness have suffered greatly and on very deep levels in recent generations. A new awakening has begun in which men are beginning to seek answers to the questions that result in massive misunderstandings among ourselves, our children, women co-workers and friends. These misunderstandings manifest themselves in rampant drug use, broken marriages, aimless careers and an unprecedented need for selective psychiatric help. Men and their inability to participate in forming working relationships lies, I believe, behind the problems inherent in rising suicides, family breakup, the ability of American corporations to compete successfully in world trade, and is blocking our national potential for greatness.

Perhaps the most damaging aspect of this problem is an overwhelming sadness I have found in men about their condition. We are not happy about not knowing how to communicate with our women and with one another. We are not happy about not being able to freely access our emotions, and less happy with the results when we do. Mostly, however, we are just sad and don't know why, but even worse we don't know what to do about it.

Men are beginning to learn that the results we create in our lives *are* what we *want*, but only a small measure of *who we are*. Those wants that manifest our reality come from deep unconscious patterning and may be far different from what we *think* we want. The unconscious mind exercises its might through the ego, and when put to the test will win 100 percent of the time, until we begin to fight back. Knowing who we are is the goal, and it is accessing that "knowing" that sets up our lessons and defines the problems we will experience. The results we create are a function of how we live the process. The process is causal, changes that may occur are the result.

This is a book about men, yes. It is also a book about women, in the sense that under all the social and economic pressures, confusion, and ego based defense mechanisms with which we all live, is the basic need to be loved. Love knows no sexual exclusivity. Women today are having a serious problem understanding men, and the fault lies mutually, not separately. Men complain about women, women about men, and desperately few of us are really happy in our relationships. She is a victim of him, he blames her, and we play an ego-officiated, win-lose game of competition that can only be lose-lose in reality, because when one person wins at another's expense, no one wins. The self help, spiritual, and psychological counseling industries are booming, because people need answers. I have personally been through much of it, studied and observed as much as I could, and I believe that the answers are not hard to find. It is the process of acceptance that is difficult. I find that it all goes back to the father-son relationship for all of us. The father issues in our culture are staggering, and the effect on our lives is monumental.

I have discovered through my own pain, joy, study and experience, the immense importance that fathering has on the lives of every one of us. The complexity of our world today makes it critical that we explore the meanings of fathering at every level. Those men and women who believe that their relationship with their father is not directly tied to relationships with everyone else in their lives, and particularly to their children, are whom this book was written for.

Writing this book was not an easy task. I was compelled to live through every issue touched, to access all the wounds, and to attempt to gain levels of understanding in areas in which I was ill-prepared. I have gone from middle-class "abundance" to being homeless and pennyless. I have seen friendships disappear when my neediness dominated them. I have found beautiful and intense personal relationships when all that was left was honesty and a willingness to be me. What I have discovered is only a drop in the ocean of what is needed to be known. If, however, through this effort, I can help just a few of those men and women who are in pain, my journey will have been worth it.

This is not an easy book to read, it was meant to challenge not give easy answers. The structure starts simply and builds continuously, through reinforcement of concepts, to repattern the unconscious mind. It will bring up many issues for the reader that will not sit well. *Please consider as you read that it is from those issues to which you most strongly react or resist, that the most benefit will come.* My opinions and beliefs are unimportant. It is how they affect you, and what you choose to do about it that is important. The book is meant to stimulate, to stir up the apathetic, the satisfied, the questioning, who could have so much more in their lives, regardless of how much they already have. If the reader feels anger rising, frustration building and an under-the-surface feeling to respond in some way, then I will have done my job. It is the reader's job to respond in his/her life in a way that brings about growth.

Man or Woman, it matters not what we are called, there is a father and son, friend and lover in every one of us; the young one looks up for answers, the elder looks down for questions. Somewhere, in the space between, they meet and become one. The parent and the child, each the source for the self and the other.

And a woman who held a babe against her bosom said,
Speak to us of children.

And he said:
Your children are not your children.
They are the sons and daughters of Life's
longing for itself.
They came through you but not from you,
And though they are with you
yet they belong not to you.
You may give them your love
but not your thoughts,
For they have their own thoughts.
You may house their bodies but not their souls,
For their souls dwell in the house of tomorrow,
which you cannot visit, not even in your dreams.
You may strive to be like them,
but seek not to make them like you.
For life goes not backward nor tarries with yesterday.
You are the bows from which your children
as living arrows are sent forth.
The archer sees the mark upon the path of the infinite,
and He bends you with His might
that His arrows may go swift and far.
Let your bending in the archer's hand be for gladness;
For even as he loves the arrow that flies,
so He loves also the bow that is stable.

kahlil gibran

...there is no difference between loving your wife, your children and all of mankind. The elements of perceived success and failure are the same.

Author

INTRODUCTION

Across America and around the world women are rediscovering their power in a way that is changing the lives of their men, be they fathers, sons or husbands. In the sixties and seventies it was Liberation. In the eighties it's called *Self Identity, Awareness,* or the *New Age.* Whatever the label, and whatever our position on the subject may be, for many men it's *trouble,* and just maybe, if we choose, *opportunity.*

In **MAN IN TRANSITION,** we will look at how a positive working balance can occur in all male relationships through understanding the essence of maleness as represented in the father-son relationship. Volumes of literary work exist on "how to" from a woman's point of view, but very little is found on how the male can best cope with the developing feminine power structure, and the even more important question of how this power relates to the young male role modeling process. This last subject is one that is as deeply significant to women as to men themselves.

Concepts explored in this book are based on the father/son relationship and how it can set the standard for *all* relationships, and develop a balance allowing unconditional love, understanding and compassion. What is important is less who the relationship is with, than how we hold the concept of relationship itself. We will probe not the results as much as the processes. We will see that husband and wife, father and son, mother and daughter, employer and employee, although each unique and separate, are part of the same overall inter-relationship.

Herein lies a not so secret elixir that can, if acknowledged and properly administered, enrich and reward us beyond our conscious desires and wildest hopes and dreams, with ramifications affecting the survival of the planet itself. In the final analysis, it is all up to us. *We are in choice about our lives.*

As a boy, raised in the heat of World War II, my world was colored and shaped in a way vastly removed from that in which my sons were raised. In fact, the view that these past forty years have witnessed the creation of greater forward movement in human development than all the preceding years in total is quite easy to support.

My own sons reached their teens in suburban Washington D.C., being the only kids they knew, living with both natural parents. Everyone else it seemed had multiple sets of parents and it was not unusual to have six or eight grandparents! In my own case, my father died when I was eight years old and my mother never remarried, choosing to raise my sister and myself with honor and respect without help from anyone.

I was the result of a tough, determined and fiercely independent mother and no real father figure to teach me my lessons. Thus it began for me, and through this book my pleasure and opportunity will be to share with you some of these lessons. They are based on an unyielding faith in the potential of the human race, a passionate love for my sons, the land, and an absolute trust that we are not alone.

As I was growing up, I was never really aware of the fact that there was no male role model in our family. I had John Wayne, Hopalong Cassidy and Roy Rogers. Because none of them ever had to deal with a woman needing to express her freedom, it never occurred to me that I would have to. Their women always seemed to fit the perfect stereotype: hardworking, true, not too smart and usually subservient to a powerful male who always got the girl and came home from war a hero.

My kids began their TV "education" during Vietnam, where rugged maleness and the proud valor of human sacrifice were supported on the nightly news by protests and anti-war demonstrations. These protests involved many groups, among them women who, in the midst of their own identity and self-awareness struggle, adopted a platform that would express their own internal angers as well as denounce an unjust war.

In the 50,000 years or so that man has been on earth in some recognizably familiar form, maleness has been a simple and obvious quality. Only in the past 200 years or so has there been confusion about this issue, and only in the past fifty has it become a major challenge to our survival. During the next twenty it will become critical.

For centuries sons literally walked in their father's footsteps across the fields. Men measured themselves against the flags and valor of bravery in war. Man survived by being instruments of death. Only the strongest survived to procreate and protect his family. For woman, male strength became synonymous with the ability simply to survive. The twentieth century seemed to be preparing mankind for a different message.

We have seen created a massive shock factor that has pulled the pins out from under centuries of masculine psyche development. From the mass annihilation witnessed as modern warfare exercised its birthright in the bloody trenches of World War I, culminating in WWII with the destruction of Hiroshima and Nagasaki, the times presented their message. Then came the Korean War and the experience of the fanatical mindset of the Oriental warrior, only to be rediscovered in Vietnam. The wanton death and destruction encountered in Southeast Asia were so unnatural to the American ideal that we ended up fighting our own internal wars as much as the Viet Cong.

As though the Vietnam experience itself were not enough to foretell the changes coming, we had more: unprecedented changes in human-rights awareness, again ripping away at centuries of traditional social structure; the assassinations of the Kennedy brothers and Martin Luther King, further reinforcing general insecurity and emphasizing our vulnerabilities as men.

The net effect brought up an evolutionary, conceptual confusion about what maleness was and should be. On the one hand, we had been conditioned to believe that fighting for one's country should be the highest form of valor, but as a result of our efforts in Vietnam, we saw the women we loved propelling disgust, anger and resentment at us and what we viewed as our qualified maleness. *And many of us agreed with them.* Men in government were consistently objects of ridicule for the administration's no-win policy and unwillingness to take responsibility for what was obviously a huge disaster in the minds of most Americans and the world. Then came the final blow of a nearly impeached President, subconsciously implanting a condemnation of the integrity and ideals of male leadership. Of course there were still many heros and those performing at extraordinary levels, but they somehow seemed to get lost in the mix of media sensationalism. The seeds of shattered male ego, self-image and the resultant vulnerability were being reinforced deeply in the psyches of American men and women.

Today, in the late 1980's, we are entering an entirely new era of human consciousness. Our expansion as a species is demanding rapid new growth just to assimilate what has recently been created. The Vietnam war was a male war, as have been all wars throughout history. Few, if any, did as much damage to the human condition that Vietnam did. No one escaped the lessons, and my belief is that its greatest lessons are perhaps yet to be learned. These lessons will be felt most in what is called the area of human consciousness or awareness of man in relationship to himself and his world. A new world of consciousness is forming and the father-son relationship must be at the front line of awareness to lead us into it. This new world will encompass not only our family and friends, but our interaction with all of mankind and the level of responsibility that we accept for their well being.

As we have seen, the results of movements taken place during this century have created a condition in which the male ego has taken a severe beating. We need to look not at repairing the ego to historical patterns, but at creating new understandings of the way in which the ego works for and against us.

Our attention needs to be focused not on recovering past glories, but on understanding how we fit into the world we have created and chosen to live in. With understanding comes growth, and growth is the only real path to happiness.

Here is presented a progression of ideas, objectives and practical techniques to develop, through the core relationship of the father and son, an understanding of what makes relationships work. *All relationships*. My premise is that there is no difference between loving your spouse, your children and all of mankind. The elements of potential success and failure are exactly the same. Because of the time and place we have reached in human development, it is critical to the survival not only of mankind, but of the planet itself, that we look at our relationships in a vital new way.

For the first time in modern history, a new movement of energy is being defined, which is an underlying current in this work. This impetus is called *expanded feminine energy awareness, or "The Feminine Principle"*. A prime component is the belief that, based on results, the male has proven he is not capable of creating a lasting peace in the world, and that women have been charged by divine province to expand the feminine energy influence to accomplish what men have been unable to achieve. Recent significant growth in what is called "New Age" belief systems is one element of support for this phenomenon. We will spend considerable time in these chapters looking at what this expanded feminine energy means, and how it will affect our lives.

Here, the discussion must turn to the concept of male vs female "energy," as opposed to "gender," discussed later. The issue is the balance of male/female energies in each of us, not necessarily the sex of the body. This is a spiritual, or universal energy that has been understood in varying degrees in most cultures since the beginning of time. Nationally, as well as world wide, people in ever enlarging numbers, are moving in their spiritual understanding to acceptance of the basic, and simple fundamental tenets upon which all great religions have been built, but which seemingly have become lost over the thousands of years of organized religious activity. These belief systems are based on an acceptance of the One God principle, and that all things are part of that One God energy, man being only one manifestation of that energy. This recent spiritual awakening may or may not be greater than during other periods of history, but the willingness of Americans, in ever increasing numbers, to flow in this direction for their answers to the meaning of life is noteworthy. It is within this spiritual context that one can most easily understand the concept of divided but inseparable energies.

We will take a closer look at these symptoms and the way they affect our lives as the chapters develop. What is important here, as it relates to this discussion, is the observation that more women are moving in this direction, and to a far greater degree than are men. Organizers of self help, and spiritual seminars and retreats, as well as workshops of many kinds, have found a consistent pattern of attendance - that being 75% to 80% are women. There are a number of reasons why this may occur, but what is important is that the American male become aware that women appear determined to find their answers with us or without us.

If we as men are to be fully effective and productive in our lives and in our relationships, we must become aware and active in the sensitive areas of our being, that which we will investigate as our "feminine side." The name of the game is actually world peace and survival, and it requires human relationships that work, and work well. Men have a tendency to be far more resistant to looking at other possibilities that may exist for them, than do women. This is evident in the importance that women play in the decision making factors in all aspects of men's lives, from handling the home finances to setting up the social calendar. Our seemingly innate male resistance to exploring alternate possibilities, has taken us and our world to a place that appears to be operating out of balance. The expanding awareness of feminine energy has been the natural evolution of this imbalance. It is evident, however, that this energy is unfocused in its intention and direction.

This energy imbalance exists in all our relationships, but is most sensitive within the nuclear family. *I will move freely back and forth in the following chapters between the parent and child/husband and wife relationship, because as you will see, they are inseparable, and in fact subject to the same dynamics.*

We have a wonderful opportunity and responsibility to share in the creating and nurturing of a world that works, without the threat of a nuclear cloud over us. The first step is to look at our relationship with our sons and fathers. It is the sons who will fight the future wars or make the future peace. Based on current world conditions, we truly have no sensible choice but to make this choice positively and immediately. If we don't we're going to lose it all. The good news is that everything we need to know about relationships with women, other men, superiors, peers and employees, is inherent in the father/son relationship. The bad news is that unless we take action to guide men into this new awareness, we are doomed as a species.

*No problem can be solved from the same
level of consciousness that created it.*

Albert Einstein

HISTORICAL TIME LINE

The time line is used for a sense of perspective in the development of man as a species in relation to his world. Obviously the time line presented here could not be reproduced in accurate scale, because it would require reams of paper. It is shown to impress the reader with the graphic awareness of how rapidly the human race has developed in recent times, as compared to the age of the planet. This graphic is referred to several times in the book to emphasize specific points.

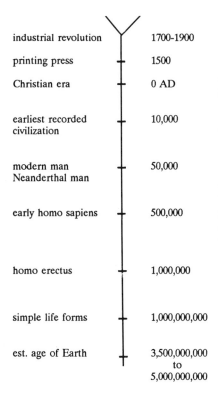

Based on the estimated age of the planet at 5 billion years, the time in which man has been present represents a percentage that is literally too small to calculate in a meaningful way. (Approx. .001 percent)

Substantially all of our art, philosophy and technology hasbeen created within the past 500 years. We are now creating new information at a rate so fast, it is estimated that 97% of all knowledge that will exist at our death will not have been known at our birth.

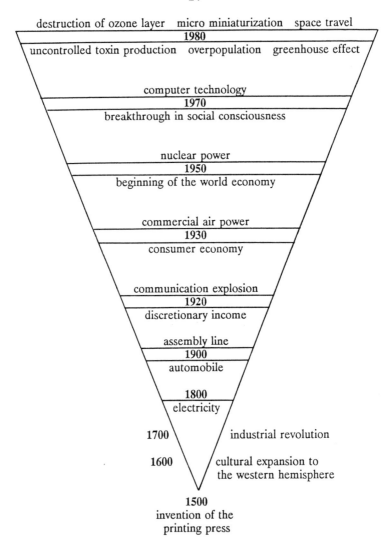

With the advent of the printed word, man became socially and culturally unlimited. The brain began to expand at a rate never experienced on the Earth plane. By the industrial revolution this growth had reached mathematically exponential proportions. We have just begun to examine our potentials for growth.

PART ONE - DEFINING THE PROBLEM
MY OWN STRUGGLE

When my father died I was eight years old, and the Readers Digest was the most read and relied upon source of general information in the country. My mother read it like the Bible. At the time, the late nineteen forties, the Digest presented the dominant psychological thought of the time that it was best to spare a child the pain of the death of a parent.

It happened that I was away for the summer when Dad had his heart attack and so Mom decided to not have me back for the funeral. I did not get a chance to say goodbye, to experience the loss, or to grieve for him. To save me the pain, the Digest said, it would be best to remove all pictures, all personal items, in fact denude the house of all memories of my lost father. Mom dutifully complied, thinking she had done the right thing. When I arrived home almost a month later everything of his was gone, and we didn't talk much about it. We even moved shortly after I got back. I was thirty eight years old before I cried for his loss, forty before I got to say goodbye to him. I spent most of my life never getting to feel grief or pain or sorrow ...or love. In fact, I got very clearly that to grieve was painful and that as the "Man of the house now," I was to be brave, strong and anything but a sad eight-year-old. What I also got was that grief was not something a man should experience, so I dissociated from that pain and grief and in the process from *all* feeling of pain and grief. The problem is that when emotions are lost selectively, we lose not only the "negative" ones but the sensitivity to all emotion. We cannot choose to lose certain emotions; we shut down the process of cmotionality. It always comes back to haunt us. We lose our emotionality by tightening up inside, by closing down and never learning to express our feelings. Emotions can never be ignored, they can only be repressed, shoved deeper and deeper until they explode. That is one of the wonders of our humanity.

I grew up strong and positive with a determination and drive that looked a lot like compulsiveness. Some called it hyperactivity, some called it directed focus. What I know now is that it was always a tireless effort to find my father.

In effect it becomes what is called a co-dependency. Co-dependency is an addictive nature usually associated with chemical dependencies, but is always the result of dysfunctional families, and is emotionally centered. We need that insensitivity to our emotions to survive, or at least we believe we do. I fed my co-dependency by marrying a woman with a father issue as strong as mine. She had not lost her father in the physical sense, but was instead born of a man who never shared himself at all. He was a wonderful man in many ways but just was never able to express his own emotions. For twenty-three years my wife and I struggled to create a relationship on a mutually co-dependent father absence, me seeking my father-based lack of emotional sensitivity through her femininity, and the media-generated archetypes of male/female mythology. She sought hers through my masculine strength and the same set of fairy tales. It is a trap that is suicidal. The issues are family dysfunctional issues that are endemic to our culture. We, in the traditional manner, extended the problems to both our boys, and eventually had to dissolve our marriage as part of finding our solution. What we did not do was ignore the base issues, and run out to find other partners to continue the same patterns. The solution comes not from years of therapy, but from a generation of men who are willing to look at their own dysfunctional beliefs from the perspective of self responsibility.

The term "responsibility" is one used often in this book. It is a critical understanding of process. The word itself is a combination of *"response"* and *"ability"* - *the ability to respond*. As men we must learn to be able to respond to our emotions in order to find happier, fuller lives. As women we must learn that we are in this battle together for the same reasons. We are all looking to daddy for the love we thought we never got, and we mess up our lives trying to get it. The reasons are simple. First, the search is based on a lie. Father did love us, just not the way we thought he should. *Our problem, not his.* Second no one can find anyone through someone else; not father, not self. It all comes from inner awareness. Reality, the experience of life as we experience it, is a choice. Our choice. We only need to learn how to be responsible for it.

We will not get into co-dependence in this book, as it is an issue of huge magnitude, and I cannot begin to do it justice. It is suggested, however, that the reader seek out information on this subject after reading this book. It offers a wonderful opportunity to take the next step in understanding.

*Be not afraid of growing slowly,
Be afraid only of standing still.*

chinese proverb

THE FATHER and SON HERITAGE

The male/male relationship is a highly complex and little understood interaction that will receive much more attention in the years to come. Men have traditionally felt less socially dependent than women, and have generally not believed that they required the emotional support groups that the opposite sex enjoys. As the political and sociological energy shifts continue to occur, seeking a planetary balance of Feminine and Masculine influences, this aspect of masculinity must be expected to change. To a large degree the current imbalance is cultural, rather than genetic, and as men open themselves up to the greater possibilities of love in their lives, many changes will occur for them.

Here, the problems we are concerned about in relationships have less to do with psychological influences and why they happen, than cultural influences and what to do about them as they happen. The job then is to learn to understand and ensure that these conflicts are dealt with and do not repeat themselves. History has indicated that most of us tend to be slow learners in our life lessons, making the same mistakes generation after generation. If we look at life as consisting of a continuous thread of "moments," called the "now," we can stretch our perspective a little. The past has brought us to the moment we are in, the now, and the future is what we are preparing for in this and every moment. However, neither the past nor the future actually exists in the now. Based on classical philosophic thought and ancient as well as modern religious beliefs, this concept is well suited to deal with the problems faced in contemporary society.

What we have is an opportunity in every single new moment to create exactly what we want in our lives as well as in our relationships. Basing our actions on what is true now, not on what was true in moments past, or what may be true in a future moment, will result in solutions to the problems of the now. Then we will be less likely to carry those problems into the next moment. One-on-one confrontation of issues gives this experience of the now in a way that can open any relationship and allow a flow of clear new light to come in. Nowhere is it more critical than in the father relationship. The father has been absent in our culture for too long, and the results have reached a crisis point. Men no longer know how to be fathers, sons, or friends to other men, or lovers to women. The sad truth is that in too many cases we don't have working relationships at all with our lovers, friends, children or fathers, we have adversarial "positions."

Recent research has suggested that the number of men who feel their relationship with their fathers was poor to non-existent reaches nearly 100%! These astounding statistics show the importance that this relationship has on our society, and the emotional base on which it operates. With women we find many of the same base issues confronting them in relationships as well as competing as equals in the workplace. These are based on unresolved father issues which leave them with undefined pictures of how to handle both their own masculine energy and that of the men they work and live with. Even worse is the plight of the man with a highly developed sense of his own feminine, or emotional, side.

Many American men need desperately to find an emotional base, and considering the damage that we have done to our planet in the name of survival, physical might and righteous positioning, we have far less time to do it than we might like. Cultural and social movement are expanding at such a rapid pace that when compounded by our functional advancements, (electronics, computers, robotics, etc.), the time may come within our own lifespan that human relationships may be all we have left. The rate at which we are destroying our planet's resources may give us no place to go. There won't be, for most of us, the kind of all-consuming workplace that takes the blame for not coming home until after the kids are asleep. According to projections of many futurists and economic forecasts, free time and discretionary income will continue to increase, and our kids will need stronger role models if they are to survive the coming years. They will need to create their own visions and find ways to fulfill them in an ever increasingly complex society. Their future is our now.

The quality of our communication is not what we say, but how effectively we say it. When trying to get through to another human being, to come from a place of total equality is usually best. The inner peace we will talk about is mostly a result of knowing that we are all equal, without making judgments. When we judge another we are only in reality judging ourselves. If we operate from a place of believing in absolute equality, we will quickly experience a flow of understanding develop from within. That kid next to you, the woman sleeping in the next room, the indigent on the street, are all just mirror images of what you in your complexity either are or could be.

Having considered the classically psychological point of view during the structural phase, this work is based heavily on simple human observation. The truth about 20th century father and son relationships is that they have improved substantially during the past few generations. Men have begun to make it reasonably O.K. to participate in activities such as awareness trainings and specially directed seminars that allow them to get in touch with their inner feelings and consider possibilities in their lives that were unthinkable 30 years ago. Men in their 30's and 40's are discovering that they can actually feel emotional tenderness, express love and even cry, without major physical damage. They have found that trite phrases like "I love you" can work; that touching and hugging can have wondrous results. But still, most men just don't have enough working knowledge of their own potential and power to know what to do with that awareness. This is true regardless of whom the relationship is with, and shows up in the divorce rate, impotent parent/child interaction, and national industrial productivity.

We have seen the equal rights movements and particularly the equal pay for equal work ruling of 1985, (state of Washington vs its employees union) upset a very critical element in the classic image pattern of male dominance in the workplace as well. It is not difficult to understand why USA TODAY recently reported from survey results conducted that 65% of all adult males were confused about how to treat women. Among single adult men that figure jumps to 74%! That means that nearly three out of four adult men are confused about their roles in relationships with women. If we agree, as psychologists have proven, that we tend to repeat parental patterns, 75% of our sons are going to have the same experience, with 75% of our daughters. I interviewed many "New Age" women in preparing this book (because they tend to be more willing to follow their inner knowing than most) to discover what it was that they really wanted in a man. Two things became clear. First, many women, until about age forty, still believe that "prince charming" is actually out there somewhere. Secondly, that he has all the answers to solve all of her problems, and, that she need not deal with them but needs only to wait for him to appear. *Unfortunately, many men believe it too! Pretty heavy expectations on both sides*. The so-called "sensitive new man" of the early eighties really only lasted a short while until image confusion replaced him with the macho man of the late eighties. When push comes to shove, a woman's security is still seen to exist not in her own capabilities, but as dependent on a man. Compare the number of successful men with beautiful wives to the number of successful women with gorgeous house husbands. The truth is that a majority of the successful career women in this country are single. As Warren Farrell says in his book "Why Men Are The Way They Are," *"The male success object still gets the female sex object"*.

As we now move into the final decade of the century, we find that few have any real idea about the essence of maleness. We continue to make our fathers, mistakes with our own sons and educate our daughters to expect perfection. Our media tell us we must be a success object. Tall, dark, handsome, athletic, intelligent and above all wealthy, to win the beautiful girl. So it becomes the beautiful girl who defines who we are. We clearly understand that without her we are less than we should be. It makes it hard on the male and the beautiful girl, who must not settle for less than the prince. Unfortunately, it is worse yet for the girl who is less than beautiful. She gets what she deserves, the leftovers. At least that is what the programming tells her. And guess whose programming lets him know who the leftovers are?

Another viewpoint these women agreed upon was that there are still very few men who are willing to accept the female side of their consciousness to allow the sensitivity of the inner self out. That may be true. What also *may* be true is these same women are scared to death of their own femininity and are diving into the masculine side of themselves for protection of their own sensitive ego. The figures show that the "Super Woman " of the eighties has been as equally a short-lived phenomenon as the "New Man." Most women will say they want a sensitive man, but are scared to death when confronted by one expressing vulnerability. Again, according to a wonderful series of surveys conducted by USA TODAY and reported in "Tracking Tomorrow's Trends" we see that even though more than 60% of households show both male and female working, the woman still carries the overwhelming burden of the household chores. Men are not willing to give up their stereotypical images in the fear that their weakness will create rejection in their mates, *and it generally does*. More bad news is that feminine opportunity expansion has created a substantial increase in stress both in the home and in the workplace.

The good news is that movement is being created and if we don't like life the way it is, we have an ever increasing availability of choices open to us to change our conditions. What is important here is not who's right or who's wrong, but acknowledging that each of us holds as our truth that which works for us. "That which works" does not mean that which works well, or that which does not work well. It simply means, that which allows us to operate in our daily lives from a comfortable place of low risk, high comfort. (*I ask you to consider that the previous sentence would also be a wonderful definition of non-growth.*) What we believe to be true of any subject needs to be looked at in this context if we are to grow in our lives.

Our belief systems create what we hold to be true about all the events in our lives. If we can change our belief systems, then we can change what is true for us. Many fathers and sons hold very rigid beliefs about their relationships. If these relationships are anything less than wonderful, it is probably because those involved choose to believe that there is no other way, and that idea controls the interaction. What we are seeing is our resistance to possibilities, based on our belief systems, getting in our way of having what we want. To change, we must only change what we believe to be true. Think it's tough to do? Well, just think about the times you've been driving along the highway exceeding the speed limit, or stretching the yellow caution light in the absolute **belief** that there were no police around, and within minutes you're stopped on the side of the road bathed in a red and blue aura! How quickly did you change **that** belief? Of course, negative belief systems that were created in childhood through trauma and/or continuous reinforcement do not change quite that easily, but they can be changed through conscious effort and desire. Only two things are required for this process, and they may be the most important single elements in this book:

1. A commitment to create change.
2. Taking responsibility for the commitment.

An often heard question is, "why are men so afraid of commitment?" In every relationship workshop I have ever attended or hosted, and in every discussion with groups of women it comes up. "Why won't men commit to a relationship?"

As I see it, it has less to do with commitment to relationship than to the concept of commitment in general. Think back to the time line and realize that in less than twenty years, men are being asked to reverse fifty thousand years of tradition that is locked into the cellular memory of our being. The breakdown of the traditional role models has left us on pretty shaky ground, and for most men today the whole idea of permanent commitment is frightening. It shows up in the workplace perhaps even stronger than with our love relationships. Job turnover is one of the costliest employee-related expenses a company can have. When I ran my manufacturing company I hired women wherever I could over men because experience taught me they were far more dependable. They came to work more often, were late less often, and stayed on the job longer than the average male. In a conflict situation with management, women are more apt to bring the question out in the open, men more likely to walk off the job and just quit. Much the same as we do in our primary relationships.

There is no easy answer to this problem. I believe we are facing a multi-generational solution. It is tied into personal value systems that are a result of self image, awareness and esteem. All the things that we as men get, or do not get, from our dads. What is needed is for men to start working and for women to stop complaining. We are only prolonging the agony by believing that we are victims of others' actions. Taking responsibility for our life is the only way out thus far discovered. In the following chapters you will read about commitment and responsibility in just about every subject covered. Commitment and responsible action are to wholeness as the alphabet is to the writer. Without it there is no hope.

In order to find a path that can be followed to help create these new patterns of behavior, it is necessary to visualize the process of belief system structure. Through this process, which I call "**The Growth Continuum,**" the level of consciousness is changed. Albert Einstein, himself a man of extraordinary spiritual awareness, has given the world many ideas and concepts that have changed the course of mankind. One of the most powerful yet simplest ideas was the observation, "*No problem can be solved at the same level of consciousness that created it*." Through the graphic representation below, it can be seen that this process can be applied to any activity, including relationships.

THE GROWTH CONTINUUM

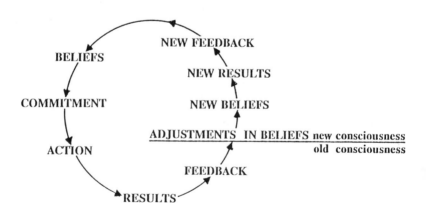

Not having had a male role model in my nuclear family, and then being blessed with two sons, has been a wonderful opportunity for me to experience and explore the joys and miseries of fatherhood. All kids must grow and test their wings within the confines of the family structure before beginning to relate to the outside world. Mine were no exception, and it took me many years to figure out that they really did not want to destroy me.

Most would agree that no relationship can be perfect all of the time, or even acceptable all of the time. To achieve balance in any relationship, which may be the best we can ever hope for, we must, by definition, have both good and bad times. Acceptance, recognition and the need for each individual to be able to express himself is the core of a well-balanced relationship. Balance is the key to operating within a context of responsibility. Creating balance comes from open communication of ideas and beliefs about what we expect from a person and what they can expect from us. Before this can be understood, however, we must begin to learn to know what to expect from ourselves. So, looking at our **beliefs** is the logical place to start.

Exploring our beliefs about the father and son heritage as a starting point will present us with the foundation for finding ways to create balance. I can assure you that it will also present an opportunity to look at how beliefs affect our relationships.

For endless generations, sons have watched while fathers spent their total waking hours providing food, shelter and basic necessities, while women handled the emotional needs of the family. These behavior patterns continued with the sons setting up their own households and extending the learned traditions. Then came the industrial revolution and suddenly the family experienced time with no attached survival need.

During the children's early years, the fathers were emotionally unavailable to suckle, fondle and support their babies, and the ability to express mutual emotion never developed. Little natural bonding developed, so that this phenomenon of free time was not well used in the development of the father and son relationship. As we progressed into the 20th century, free time became more abundant, communications of all kinds opened up and relationships began to expand. With expansion and growth come problems of adjustment, and many of these adjustment problems are with us today in acute form. These problems have given us the opportunity, as in no other time in history, to look at the quality of how we live and work with ourselves and others. It could not possibly have come at a more critical time. Survival in today's world has become a function of giving and taking. For too long man has taken from his world and given little or nothing back, that has not been poisoned or stripped of value. As a result the giving has become as difficult as the taking and in many areas of our lives we can no longer discern the difference, particularly in our relationships.

The net result is a high level of stress, worldwide, and as we have all experienced, stress is not a highly productive area to operate from for very long periods of time. Stress causes fathers to batter and assault their families, broken marriages, broken commitments in all areas of life, dependence on drugs and alcohol, denial, and governments operating in constant paranoia.

I believe that the stress created by the women's movement of the past two decades, and its extension into the next two, has and will continue to have a profound impact on history. The obvious influence of this stress for women is in their not being able to fully express their talents and abilities in the whole of their being. On the positive side, men are being forced to deal with inabilities to see themselves as sensitive, caring parents, partners and lovers. To expand our feelings outwardly and leave some sign of having been here, we must start with our sons. To teach them is to learn from them. The giving is the getting. Pretty good balance. The heritage we have brought to our sons is one filled with despair and hopelessness for many, and certainly for the planet itself it is bleak at best. The oceans are a mess, the generation of massive amounts fluorocarbons eat away at our ozone layer, waste is piling high all over the world, toxins replace nutrition in our foods, even our rain is poisoned. Our gift for being alive at this time and in this country is to have the opportunity to begin developing a new heritage. One that our sons and grandsons can fearlessly take forward with a proud smile, a hug, and a willingness to love and be loved.

Close your eyes for a moment and visualize your son or father and yourself in a place and in a way that would make *you* the most happy. Then consider what you might have to give up to make *him* the happiest. What will be the cost to you? Determine whether or not you are willing to do what it will take to create that vision. If you can, commit to the possibility with a feeling of love, not with guilt or right-wrong mindedness. All the tools you will need to create that vision will be presented for you to choose from in the following chapters. The context of this work is experiential. Each area is built on the ideas of the previous chapters and is intended to give the reader an opportunity to explore ideas and processes that will expose possibilities in his or her own life.

There are no easy answers, just as there are no easy problems. There are

26

only possibilities and choices. Our heritage to our sons and daughters will be dependent upon how willing we are to take responsibility for *our* lives. We cannot teach that which we do not understand. We cannot understand that which we do not explore, study and participate in. This book is a stepping stone to balanced awareness.

*there are reasons and excuses and hopes
and wishes and good intentions and shoulds
and coulds and woulds and if onlys and
might have beens and I trieds and results.*

*Only the results count - don't confuse "you"
with the results.*

transformational jargon

FATHER HUNGER

The term "father hunger" has been attributed to Harvard University psychoanalyst James Herzog. He used the term to apply to studies of children whose fathers were physically absent for any reason. Since then the term has come to encompass any environment in which the father role model is absent physically, or emotionally, by others such as John Ross, Samual Osherson, Daniel Levinson, and Andrew Merton.

Father hunger is, I believe, the predominant factor behind *all* relationship problems that men have, and most that women experience. It is imperative that we understand the effects of this phenomenon if we are to be able to change our results in any walk of life. The father absent syndrome is so strong that in the twenty-to sixty-year-old age bracket it affects an estimated 75 to 95 percent of the population. That includes women as well as men. Those fathers who were not role models for their sons were also not there for their daughters. The daughters grew up without getting any idea of what a man was supposed to be, or got negative information. She had a choice of either recreating the father image in her relationships in order to "make it right," which can only make it worse, or setting up a media generated composite of "Mr. Right," the genetic celebrity, which is probably even worse.

These families are termed dysfunctional, in that one or both parents are not present for a majority of the time in which the children are in the home. The organization Adult Children of Alcoholics, which deals with disorders of dysfunctional families, estimates that about 98% of all families are dysfunctional in one way or another. When we look at the jail census, divorce rates, job turnover and dissatisfaction, etc. it is easy to agree. The net results are the same; high divorce, suicides, extensive therapy requirements and drug dependence. The worst part is that it continues the heritage of weak male role modeling.

Sam Osherson states in *Finding Our Fathers*,"...the psychological absence of fathers from their families is one of the great underestimated tragedies of our times. The American man who grew up with a father who was affectionate, strong, and significantly involved in the upbringing of the children is so rare he is a curiosity."

The non-ability of many adult men to express intimacy is the result of non-fathering during infancy. By the age of three, it is generally agreed that a boy has recognized his differences from Mom, and knows he is not like her. To whom can he look for emulation if no father exists? This is my biggest argument against unmarried women who, in my opinion, make the unforgivably selfish decision to have children without a father present.

Men who have not come to grips with their own father issues and enter into family life are not much better off. A relationship in which a man cannot be truly intimate on an emotional level with his wife, cannot support a caring intimate fatherhood. The man will bring his own doubts and insecurities into the parent role and continue the expectation of the woman as dominant parent. The woman then becomes responsible for the total parenting function, as well as dealing with a man who has lost her as his primary center of focus. This creates, among other things, what I call "heavy responsibility." The fun and delight in teaching one's own procreation, in watching the wondrous gifts of delight and joy that a child brings in with him or her is lost in the interaction of angers, jealousies and unresolved conflicts. Because of the basic nature of women to mature earlier and seek answers to their problems at much younger ages, men are facing a serious dilemma.

The intimacy required to develop a meaningful love relationship between parent and child is not isolatable. Intimacy is a way of being, not doing, and is a major blockage for most men. Intimacy is a feminine energy action that needs to be expressed in all of a man's relationships if it is to be present at all, and is a major part of male wholeness. Intimacy is blocked for many reasons from guilt to shame, and always falls back to the lack of touching, fondling, talking and time spent with father. Of course there are other factors which can also affect the lack of intimacy, but the father-son relationship is primal in this area. Intimacy is the single most important factor for women in physical love, and statistically is a major factor in breaking the family union. If a man deeply believes he has never been loved by a man (father), how can he possibly love himself? Where does he learn to accept and appreciate the male energy that he is? Without self love, the task of loving another is futile. For a man to become whole, these are questions he must answer.

Women are doing their work and becoming whole, in an emotional sense. As a result they want "whole" men, and the men are still resisting, but there are cracks in the dike. Women who seek their answers through continued effort and education run a great risk of creating fear, distrust and jealousy in their relationships It is worth the gamble, however. Men will not break through until the losses hurt enough. Successful relationships are the hope and dream of almost everyone. They are not impossible, but they do take work. Male intimacy is a critical element, and is directly connected to their experience of inner peace and security.

We sit around in a ring and suppose,
But the Secret sits in the middle and knows.

Robert Frost

PEACE AND SECURITY

People come or do not come to their place of peace depending on the value placed on the quality of their life from an inner viewpoint. For many of us, peace of mind is thought to be obtainable through financial security and material wealth, and for many it is, to a point. What appears to happen, however, is that when we reach that point which represents whatever material security is for us, we find the point at which inner peace is reached seems to move. As our goals are reached, the satisfaction lasts for only a short time and then kind of "oozes" out and moves just farther enough away to be slightly beyond our grasp. However, fleeting moments do occur when completion and fulfillment are sensed, and it is in these moments that we experience inner peace. It is precisely at those same moments that we gain an intuitive understanding that at any given moment we can have anything, and as much of it as we want. We find that the reward is actually in the process of completion rather than the completion itself, and that inner peace is part of, and not the result of, the process.

No real difference actually exists between our own inner peace, our family peace and world peace. Each is merely a differing manifestation of an inner knowing that as human beings our potentials are limited only by a willingness to accept our beliefs as our limits. One of my goals in this book is to present to the reader an understanding of how interconnected the world is through relationships. This is no longer a world in which fathers and sons have unique problems. The basic problems in a simple relationship, if there is such a thing, show up everywhere in our lives.

The security we seek is not present in the "things" we collect around us, but inherent in the *process* of collecting. Security, like inner peace, is not a thing we achieve and never have to be concerned about again, but a feeling of the moment that changes as the moment changes, and as our beliefs change. Those men who were children of the depression years or spent youths in great poverty have different views of security than younger and more advantaged men. Inner peace and security are different *feelings*, but each is tied to the other. Security will be whatever we believe it to be based on or belief systems of the moment. We can set goals to achieve it, measure it and have a clear picture of what it will look like when we have it. The problem is that when we get it, it loses value to us, because there actually is no such thing as lasting security. Inner peace, on the other hand, can only be achieved through living life. There is no right way to get it, and no skills needed. It is the result of simply being who we are.

There are many parts to inner peace, and keeping our goals ever so slightly beyond our reach and living the process of reaching our goals is only one part. Another part to inner peace, whether we wish to admit it or not, is spiritual. The extent to which we participate in our spiritual beliefs is of course a personal matter, but recognition of our universal selves is an absolute requirement of true inner peace. *If we can operate from an understanding that we are all representative of the same universal energy, we suddenly become consciously aware that we are all part of another. (And therefore responsible, at whatever level we choose to accept, for one another.)* Some might call this energy "God," others "Universal Oneness," "Nirvana" or "The Christ Light". There are many names for it, but does the label matter? It is the experiencing of the oneness that will take each of us, our relationships, and eventually the planet to the maximum positive potential. *Maximum positive potential* should not be confused with perfection, but rather understood from the perspective of excellence. (We will deal with the conflict of perfection vs excellence in a later chapter) For now, however, personal excellence needs to be looked at to set the context of what follows. That context is definitely a spiritual one. It comes from an understanding of the concept of oneness, which is the bridge that can help to create better relationships. As long as we hold rigid beliefs about our separation from God and one another; as long as we view ourselves as not responsible for the conditions of the whole of mankind; as long as we see ourselves as less than sacred, we will have as our results: failed personal relationships, covert governments, beautiful human beings wasting their lives on drugs, poisoned air and water, and bigger, more expensive missile systems. All highly unproductive and directly connected. I believe that the failure of many father-son relationships is due largely to the failure of men to recognize the connection of the physical father to the Divine Father. In those societies where ancestral reverence were and are practiced, such as the Native American, social balance and harmony were the rule. Roles were clear and well defined. We have lost that definition, and with it social control. The jails are full of men with no understanding of respect for basic human rights of others because our society has allowed the family structure to break up. It is within the family structure, both the physical family and the spiritual family, that we learn to understand our divine perfection.

By looking each day at setting our own personal level of operational excellence, we become aware of what we are doing against the background of what is possible. We need to look regularly at how much we are willing to do, how far we are willing to go, in our pursuit of personal excellence. This enables us to see others in the light of *their* possibilities. This process can help convert a stalled, negative approach to life to an active, helpful and positive one; help us understand the inevitable pain and tragedies of life in the light of their intended lessons, rather than as victims of circumstance; help us to see that everything emanates from a universe in divine order, with no room for accidents. Setting and operating from the limits of our own levels of excellence allows a clear perspective from which to view the dark side of life's experiences, not as ends in themselves, but as opportunities to grow.

Many of the old religions are based on a belief that we each come into life with specific lessons, both to learn and to teach. That each event is preplanned on a soul level with each of the participants, so that all may learn their lessons. That all plan to come into life, learn their lessons, and leave, only to continue the cycle of human experience, ultimately so that we may sit as one with God. I do not know how much of this is "true," in the sense of "ultimate" truth. I have, however, come to an understanding that "truth" is exactly what we believe it to be, and that therefore there can be no limits on what is possible.

Science estimates that we actually use only 2 to 5 percent of our brain potential. The possibilities that exist within that unused portion are indeed awesome and probably for most of us outside of comprehension. We are left with only one option/choice. The need simply to learn to see our choices and take the risks required to make those choices our reality. With only a 2 to 5 percent potential for mastery, how can we know for sure what is and what is not possible? If the engine in your car were running at 2 to 5 percent of its potential, how far would it go? It might possibly get you where you want to go, but at what level of efficiency?

One of the ideas that came out of the Vietnam war was the popularization of the "domino" theory. This theory proposed that if we let Vietnam fall to the enemy, all the surrounding countries would also fall in rapid and direct succession. Applying that concept in reverse, it can be seen that the more people make positive relationships a focal point in their lives, the more people will be touched in a positive way, *but it must start with someone taking responsibility.*

America is a security conscious culture. That is why we have created a "more is better" attitude, and by looking at inner peace as something for women to seek and share with us, we are giving away our only opportunity to find it. We must draw on what we know works at this time in history, because of the rapid increase in the damage being done to the quality of man's existence. We see this not only in our relationships but also in the quality and deterioration of our natural resources, too.

The ideas and thoughts presented from here on may appear to some to be a little unusual, or to others old news. In fact, some concepts we will look at are as old as human intellectual thought. Some have been taught by Buddha, Moses, Jesus and many other great teachers, writers, poets and philosophers, as well as our own contemporary "gurus." Our planet faces enormous problems in the next century. Our fathers had only physical and emotional security to deal with. Today most of us are dealing with the results of our fathers' unknowing errors in the name of progress of mankind. Population projections for the planet are mind-boggling. The attendant problems of nutrition, housing,waste disposal, detoxification and yet unknown results of our own "progress," will require worldwide efforts to solve. The concepts of national isolationism and autonomous states no longer have validity.

As DNA is the essential building block of the living cell, relationships are the essential element of world peace. For men, it is time to come to an understanding and agreement about who we are and what we want for ourselves, our families and our world.

The principles we will be working with emphasize the necessity to achieve inner peace and knowing in order that a continuum can be established which will create a positive domino effect. We can do this with lightness and spontaneity, and **it should be fun!** For too many centuries we have duped ourselves into believing that life has to be hard and dreary, and misery is a required part of our dues. Again, this *is* a belief system, and beliefs, as we will examine, are less than fixed.

Inner peace and security begin with the simple notion that *love is contagious, and unrestricted by labels*. To be sure, there is no place in this entire work in which the words **"mother/daughter, father/daughter, mother/son, husband/ wife, boy/boy,or girl/girl,"** could not be substituted in intent for **father and son.** The father and son relationship has been the one least exposed to examination and expansion, and the one therefore with the most significant opportunity for growth. Each of us possesses two kinds of "energy." We call them masculine and feminine, and we will look at how this imagery affects our lives.

The growth continuum can be viewed as a balance scale. We attract our feminine energy awareness to the left side, our masculine energy awareness to the right side. If we allow one side or the other to remain out of balance, the whole will operate in a state of non-balance, making attainment of maximum potential impossible. Therefore, to start at the inner self is imperative, and from there to progress to the son, and then to where our own needs, wants and abilities will carry us. All that is required to make it work is for the reader to make the commitment to take the first step. Once you've done that, turn the page and jump in. The water's cold but it warms up fast!

All of my days were grains of sand
I never cared where they fell

Oh, but the days that wait for me now
have something different to tell

Tomorrow lies in the cradle
Tomorrow has eyes that shine
Tomorrow lies in the cradle
with a smile a little like mine.

this is my son, my newborn son
and he's bound for a brand new day
perhaps I can walk along with him
a little part of the way.

Tomorrow lies in the cradle
Tomorrow has eyes that shine
Tomorrow lies in the cradle
with a smile a little like mine.

bob gibson

BELIEF SYSTEMS

As discussed throughout Part I, the belief systems we all operate from dictate our truth. The level of understanding that we have about our lives at any given moment is the paradigm within which we operate. A paradigm is a level of understanding from which we operate. To shift a paradigm is to move to another level of awareness or consciousness. Truth is only truth within its own paradigm, and as we grow we move into new paradigms of understanding. Capitalism is no less true than communism, Christianity no less true than Islam, given the support structure for each. It is that structure we must understand if we are to effect change in our lives. Men have a natural resistance to adjusting our belief systems, much more so than do women. Women may have more controlling beliefs than men, but are quicker to drop or change them. There are other reasons for this resistance, but they can no longer serve as excuses. Prime among those reasons is the knowledge that men and women operate inherently from different hemispheres of the brain-men being predominantly "left brained," women predominantly "right brained." Admittedly we know relatively little about the actual processing of information in the brain, but we are learning more every day. What we do know is that each hemisphere communicates on different levels. It is also known that these tendencies can be developed and enhanced. We will discuss the left/right brain influences in greater depth in later chapters, but it is important to keep these basic ideas in mind as we look at how belief systems are organized and how they operate.

My work in the study of men and communication has convinced me that although women are not absolved by any means, communication is an enormous male problem. We don't talk to our women in ways that they are able to understand what we want, we don't talk to our children in ways that they achieve a meeting of their needs, and we don't talk to ourselves, because we don't know how. By not knowing how to present our needs, we do not learn how to listen to others. Women, because of their right-brained emotional connection, *interpret* information on a feeling level. It is on this feeling, emotional level, that real communication takes place. The rest is merely a sharing of ideas. An easy argument is that not all communication needs to be felt. I have been told that "emotions have no place in the business world." Nothing could be further from the truth, because in selling, and all business is selling at various levels, we know that a person decides to buy a product or idea on an emotional level. We may not be aware of it, but if we don't feel good about an idea or product, we usually don't buy it. When we do, we end up being sorry for it, because it won't meet our needs. Business deals that come from a totally left-brained, logical, analytical place are generally the ones in which people are ultimately hurt, losses incurred, and the growth continuum impeded. With women this becomes a two-edged sword because all too often when a man makes a logically based left-hemisphere comment it is interpreted from an emotional environment and the results can be disastrous. Communication cannot take place under these conditions.

For men who cannot sustain a relationship with a woman, or who have kids with ineffective or under utilized potentials, drug and alcohol related problems, this is a key area to look at. Success, like truth, is relative. The truly successful man will be equally at peace as friend, parent and in the workplace. Our male heritage has not made this an easy task.

To a great number of men, the workplace has become a haven to escape the emotional bedlam he faces at home. He goes there to avoid the confusion and feeling of impotence of not knowing how to communicate. Unfortunately, what he is beginning to discover is that we are pretty much the way we are with everyone. We can playact for a while, but our personalities are non-exclusive. In my corporate workshops we often find technically excellent workers who are promoted because of their knowledge and performance, and who then find they know absolutely nothing about managing people. What we discover in working with them is that there is almost always a carryover in that lacking to their personal lives. Effective management, as well as effective personal relationships, requires a deep sense of understanding of how people access and respond to information. The same understanding we can get from exploring our relationships with our fathers and sons.

It will be difficult for many men reading this to go farther. What will come up is a recognition of ideas on an intellectual level, but a fear that it may actually be true on a heart level. It is the resistance to growth showing up, and it is a fear of change. Here is where the work begins, and to do that, let's take a look at what these belief systems are that control us so completely.

In his landmark book, *The New Male*, Dr. Herb Goldberg details the stages that men typically follow through a lifetime. I have paraphrased his remarkably on target observations to point up how desperately men are controlled by their belief systems.

Ways the male sees himself

ALIVE AT TWENTY
A MACHINE AT THIRTY
BURNED UP AT FORTY

At Twenty	At Thirty	At Forty
Urgently sexual.	Sexually mechanical.	Sexually anxious.
Restless, Passionate, Eager	Conservative, appropriate.	Holding on, maintenance of place (Hanging on.)
Physically active, open for action	Exercising purposefully	Fear motivated compulsiveness.
Playful, curious, adventurous.	Entertainment limited and controlled.	Passive, reluctant to leave TV.
Optimist, boisterous, laughing.	Pragmatist, realist	Cynical, snickers, rarely laughs.
Buddyship, many close	Guarded around other men.	Few male relationships.
Blunt, honest, rude, direct	Appropriately tactful, manipulative and phony.	Not knowing what he feels or even believes.

These archetypes are the result of belief systems about who we are at different stages of experience. It is easy to note how constrictive and restrictive men's attitudes become as we get older.

Belief systems are the result of conscious and subconscious input that bombard our systems from the moment of birth (some would argue even before), to the day we die. On the following page is diagramed a graphic interpretation of how this system inter-relates with how we see our world. I have structured this analysis to show how we process the information available to us. This subject alone could absorb volumes of work, and I have attempted to simplify it to basic concepts.

At the core, or center of the form we call "life" is the self. It is composed of an undefined energy. That God connected pureness that some would call the soul. Here, where even the most pragmatic of physicists now agree, lies the true essence of mankind as a species. Here resides our true knowing of who we are, without judgment or right/wrong mindedness. Surrounding this core are an unlimited series of layers. The first we can call the unconscious mind, where all automatic functions of the body are controlled. It requires, and in fact accepts, little interference with its DNA programing, and it appears to be untouchable by outside programming. In computer terminology the self might be said to be analogous to the hardware.

The next layer we will call the subconscious mind. This may operate like a transition layer in which certain choices of action are made. It is probably here that hypnotism and subliminal suggestion becomes effective, and is largely right brain controlled. The study of Neuro-Linguistic Programming has uncovered many layers within these first two bands that can affect our reactions to our environment. I believe that this is where all psychological therapies react, and is the area over which we have the most control for behavioral change and attitudinal manipulation. It can be seen, in fact, as being made up of many layers itself, each more dense and less impenetrable as it gets closer to the unconscious. This could be thought of as the computer's software.

The third layer, the conscious mind, is also complex, but far less dense and totally malleable, and is directly connected to the sensory collectors. Here is where our decisions come from, where all choice is made, where education and experience is processed and distributed throughout the system. The analogy here would approximate the function of the keyboard.

Somewhere between the conscious and subconscious resides memory, and likewise between subconscious and unconscious lies ego. Around all of this are continuous bands of what we will call filters. These are the experiences of life that give us our attitudes, prejudices, fears and expectations. They start in the birth canal and color the way we see our world, and the way the world sees us. Literally everything that comes within the awareness of our senses is absorbed here, most of which we never even know about. When we talk about change, what we are really talking about is removing these filters. This is really about all that can be changed, without deep therapy, and even that is up for grabs. The belief systems we operate from reside fully within these filters, and in Part II of the book, we will be dealing with many of the components of them, one by one.

If you are reading between the lines, you may have gotten the message that the *who* that we are, we will always be. We cannot change who we are outside of chemical attack on the DNA. We can only change what we believe to be true about ourselves and our relationships, by examining our beliefs. This is the premise from which all motivational training programs are developed. It is really very simple. We need only to recognize that our lives and relationships could be better, more fulfilling and rewarding, that we have a responsibility like at no other time in history to impact the future of the world, and then commit to do something about it.

The Anatomy of Belief Systems

Outside influences in the form of everything that comes into contact with us through the sensory system is absorbed into the self. First, however, it must pass through a complicated system of controlling filters made up of past experiences. By the time each aspect of each piece of information is processed through the various layers, it is changed to conform to the path of least resistance in our lives. It is only the outer layer that can be effectively changed on a conscious level. We have little control over the outside influences, and the mind processes are genetically sealed. Only the filters are of our own making and only we can change them. It is important to note that as the information is colored as it passes through the filters, so also it is colored as it comes back through them on the way back out. That is why it is so difficult for us to see possibilities and also why others often don't see things the way we do.

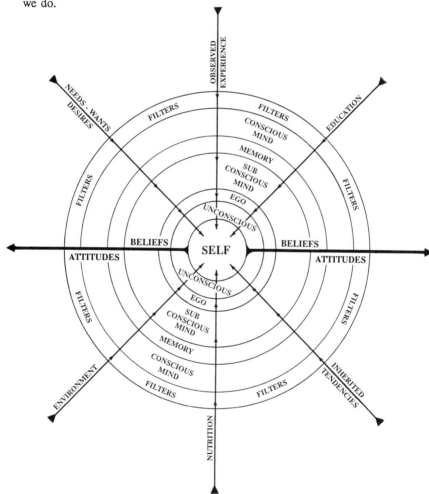

PART II

PART II - THE TOOLS

TOOL #1
COMMUNICATION

The many areas we will touch in this section require some basic understanding in order to weave together into a sensible whole. It seems natural to start with a basic discussion of the golden thread that holds all the various parts together, communication.

Ask any three women what the biggest single problem with men is, and at least two will say, "They don't know how to communicate." Most men do know *how*, they just don't.

What is true is that there is a vast communication problem between men and women, men and men, and to a substantially lesser degree, women and women. It does appear that when a male is involved in a conversation with a woman, there is a greater chance of misinformation than when the conversation is between two men or two women. We must, however, consider that the problem is not necessarily a male problem, but a uniquely natural, understandable and *correctable* condition of basic neurological differences between how men and women process information. We will have to examine in depth our beliefs about those differences, however, if we are to make any changes.

Neuro-Linguistically, words have very different meanings to each of us, depending on many factors such as education, background, etc. We know for example that as much as 85% percent of our communication is received unconsciously from other than verbal input. Such factors as eye movement, voice, body posture, physical gestures, and many others, can subconsciously sabotage the most thoroughly prepared presentation of ideas. This happens because we perceive the body language along with the auditory input, and filter it through our systems based on that which we already believe to be true.

A major element in effecting our belief systems is understanding how the brain accesses information. Basically humans understand their sensory input in three ways; visually, auditorially or kinesthetically. (There are others, but these are the primary ones.) All are present within each of us, but one will always be dominant, particularly under conditions of stress. To communicate effectively with the visual person, one must develop mental pictures for him or her. The auditory requires hearing the information, and the poor kinesthetic won't understand a word you say unless he/she can "feel" or relate to it on a personal basis. Herein lies one of the basic problems in understanding relationships.

At the base of the processing structure, hidden deeply beneath the conscious surface, are our childhood emotional bondings. The roots of emotional bonding go so deep in the father/child relationship that often the intensity is equal to that encountered in a primary love relationship. The difference is that the primary love relationship is very close to our active consciousness and the father/child relationship is buried so deep that it often has a polarizing effect. On a very simplistic level, this is why we often seek our parents in our mates, repeat our parents' behavior patterns with our own children, and why it is often the ones closest to us who are the most difficult to communicate with. It can also be easily seen why it is so vital that we stop the cycle of non-communication. When we are involved in these kinds of intensive communication efforts, regardless of how close to the surface they may be, we revert to our natural, primary information accessing system.

The problem is that when two people are using different systems, communication becomes very difficult. A way must be found to get both parties accessing from the same system, or modality. Generally it is most effective for both parties to switch into the kinesthetic modality, which is where real listening becomes possible.

I am a high auditory. For twenty-three years I was married to a high visual (which is not unusual, by the way.) It is interesting to note how often we unconsciously choose mates who balance our weaknesses. Every time we became embroiled in an argument, it would end the same way. She would say something like, "You can never *see* my point of *view*," and I would retort a little louder, "You just don't *listen* to a word I *say*." We expressed ourselves in the primary accessing modes that were natural to us. I must hear things to make sense of them. I talk a lot, read out loud to myself and constantly have an internal dialogue going on inside my head that I listen to. I ask myself literally thousands of questions daily and answer them. She, on the other hand, makes sense of her world by creating mental images or pictures. She sees her input, and when she gets information in a verble mode and cannot convert it into pictures, she goes into trance. There was simply no way one could get the other to communicate until the discussion got to a kinesthetic level. When it got so frustrating that we would both begin to cry is when the work could begin. One of the reasons Gestalt therapy is so successful in transpersonal work is that it allows direct accessing of the feeling state. The words we use in normal conversation, specifically the predicates and predicate phrases, give away the accessing system being used.

What actually happens is the brain goes into trance when it is not operating in its primary representational modality. When we find ourselves saying the same things over and over to our kids, or anyone, without receiving the appropriate response, it may well be that their brains are simply not "hearing" words that they readily recognize. It becomes our responsibility to develop a languaging system that works to achieve the goal we want. It is important to know what the representational modalities are of those in our close relationships because these are the areas in which communication is most important.

(This information is based on the science of Neuro-Linguistic Programming, generally known as NLP. It is a subject of great depth, and like many of the ideas presented here, will require additional study to become effective as a tool. We will discuss many aspects of NLP throughout the book, but they will not be labeled as such, in the interest of staying focused.)

As if that weren't enough, there is another built in detour to effective communication that is becoming increasing better understood. This is the fact that we humans happen to have two separate halves to our brains, and each of the sexes is predominantly opposite.

The male is predominantly "left-brain" oriented, while the female operates naturally out of the right hemisphere. The difficulty lies in the emotional implications of these differences. Each side will react differently to the manner in which words are used, in addition to the words themselves. It is all interpretation until we learn to speak the same language. We will deal with this aspect in greater detail in the following chapters. What is important now is for the reader to begin to get the idea that effective relationships have nothing to do with the people in the interaction, but in the way we and they communicate our wants and needs. As long as we must interpret, we are not communicating. Learning to say what we mean, asking for what we want, is a process that will take time and a committed effort to create, but it is the only thing that will work.

Another NLP subject of much value is the area of body language. Much has been written and said about body language, but it is in my opinion a very difficult art. The brain processes information on so many levels that it is difficult to use a narrow tool to make assumptions about another's behavior, so we must use tools that access multiple levels of brain activity. This is where the viewer's belief systems get in the way and again we must deal with interpretation rather than sensory-based input. By sensory-based input, I mean experiencing reactions through our sensory elements: the eyes, ears, fingers, etc.

In teaching NLP, one of the most useful tools I use is watching facial expressions. Most of us are totally oblivious to the movement of muscles and changes in skin tone in the person with whom we are engaged. By learning to watch closely what is happening physically, two things happen. First we get to drop out of our own considerations and agendas about that person and be alive and in the moment with them. For most of us that is an unusual experience. We automatically focus our eyes on them to see what is happening and just that contact alone makes a difference to both the sender and receiver. Maintaining eye contact is a terrific way of communicating and very difficult for most people. Watch those people in your life who you feel are good communicators, and the odds are overwhelming that they will have good eye contact habits.

The second thing that happens, of course, is that after some practice you will begin to notice how your communication is being received. What is heard and what passes through. A simple and fun test of this will spark your awareness. Find a mirror with good lighting. Stand in front of it and make very slight adjustments in the eyes, eyebrows, nose, lips, etc. Notice how much information you can project through these subtle movements. Widen and narrow the eyelids, in the smallest possible degrees. See how many feelings you can express without words. Also note how much you miss without looking directly into your own eyes.

Remember, our unconscious knows all this stuff. We have forgotten it, but the unseen mind will make judgments for us based on this kind of input. The problem is we are not in control of it. Becoming sensitive to these kinds of observable reactions opens up all our sensitivities, and puts us in a place of choice. As we will see, it is this gift of choice that opens the floodgates of joy and success in life. Without a recognition of the importance of communication in the total structure of a relationship, there is no way that we can effectively discuss the other components that follow.

It would seem on the basis of the foregoing that male/male relationships would be easy for men, given their similar tendencies. On the level of potential this is true; unfortunately however, there are other factors that block that reality. We will look at them under the headings of Risk, Fear and Rejection.

Communication can be looked at as a continuous loop, in which party A sends a message, party B receives it, and then feeds it back to party A in a way A understands that B understands it. Anything else is just sharing, and not worthy of building anything on.

As you read on, just be aware that each segment of the book is designed to fit together using the golden thread of communication to tie it together. What you will discover as you become more conscious of communication as a specific part of your relationships is that it will automatically get better and better. There are many courses and books available to help, but there is no need to do anything other than just be aware of the interaction around you to get an awareness of the possibilities that exist.

In Part I, we had the opportunity to briefly look at the larger picture of relationships in order to build a background of understanding. In Part II we explore the realities of applied action to solve specific relationship problems. These are the tools of the relationship trade. Much of what follows is the result of my own, non-clinical work over the past few years, and from my corporate and couples workshops. It is all based on concepts that lead to happier, healthier lives. However, this is only a beginning, and part of the responsible action that must be taken is for the readers to take those ideas that "feel right" to them and continue to develop them through additional workshops, reading and discussion groups.

One of the most effective ways of doing this is through the formation of men's issues groups. I have formed several of these groups and find them to be the most positive way to get involved in looking at and sharing common questions and ideas.

Recommended guidelines for forming such groups can be had at no cost by writing the author.

I would hope that you, the reader, might use the margins to make notes as you read through the chapters. Note your *emotional* responses as you read. Put down your *feelings* as they come up, as well as questions that occur to you. When you've completed the book, page back through and see if your questions have been answered. The chapters have been structured to build awareness and understanding, and the level of available information for you to draw on at the end will, I hope, be greater than at the beginning. If you find that there are areas that have not been sufficiently answered for you, I invite you, again, to write to me.

happiness is a mans greatest achievement:
it is the response of his total personality
to a productive orientation toward himself
and the world outside.

Eric Fromm

TOOL #2

UNCONDITIONAL LOVE

Everyone probably would agree that we all love our children. To stop and define that love may take a little more thought. Love moves along a jagged line, sometimes plentiful, sometimes less so, depending on the circumstances. Kids are very sensitive to this movement and respond in erratic ways in reaction to the flow of emotion perceived coming to them. Love is the foundation of security, and the way we relate to others is dependent on our own sense of security. *Unconditional love is love that exists for us regardless of expectations, performance or results.* When a child fails at a task and feels that his parents will therefore love him less, he will attempt to cover up his failures in one way or another. In society today, a young person's peer group acceptance is vital to his existence, particularly today, with the parental authority figure having become either benign or negative. The peer group is where much of the teen's security exists, and I can think of few shakier places for a kid to have to go to find his security. Indeed, it is the unusual child who marches to his own drummer without regard for how he is accepted by his contemporaries. As children enter the teen years, failure to meet parental expectations is almost always of less importance than failure to achieve peer approval. Kids will take the risk of being in trouble at home over group disfavor because they know that sooner or later it will normalize at home, but the instant gratification of peer acceptance is only available in the moment. Children instinctively know and appreciate the beauty of spontaneity, or living in the moment, but like many other qualities, society educates it out of them, often for budgetary reasons. We will spend much more time on the concept of living in the moment in later chapters. The more secure a youngster feels about his position, the more logic and common sense will come into play in the decision-making processes. When critical decisions come up in their lives, they should be making them based on a balance of firm data and emotional responses. Spontaneity can only come from a feeling of security. Knowing that they will not be judged good or bad, right or wrong, in the sense of their totality. They can and will do *things* that are good/bad, right/wrong, but we must learn to see *them* separately from what they do.

The vital link in a working father and son relationship is **unconditional love.** Internal, as well as external, open communication is the process through which it can be attained. By that I mean we must know our own intention internally before we can communicate it to someone else. Through this communication process both collect data about who they are and what is expected. When a child knows that his position as a loved and appreciated part of the family structure is not up for renegotiation, **under any circumstances,** he can operate from a solid center in his life. If love is not tied to specific performance, the child can approach his tasks from a position of knowing that all that is at stake is his level of performance at that task. It then becomes a simple learning experience, not complicated by non-productive emotional investment, usually called *anger.* The parent, conversely, must be constantly aware on the intuitive as well as practical level, of what is going on in the child's life. For the man with younger children, this process of being involved in the moment will begin an opening of emotional feelings that once experienced can be denied, but not forgotten. It will spread to all other relationships as long as the desire and commitment to do so are there. Our children can be counted on to give us immediate and honest feedback. If you don't like what you're getting from them, there is only one place to look for correction: inside, to your own motivations and feelings. The same thing, of course, is true of all people we are in contact with.

Most of us take for granted that just because we say something to someone, we have communicated with them. If that were the case, there would be no need for this book. What most of us do most of the time is simply share, with no real knowledge of the effectiveness of the communication. Few of us have ever learned *really* to listen, and therefore have no way of knowing if we are communicating or not. The only way we find out is by our results, and then, of course, it's too late. The results are the feedback we get, and if we interact with others in the actual moment, that is, *we are totally present in the experience with them,* we can read that feedback instantly. Men spend so much time being driven by the competitive need to succeed that we have no time to listen to the feedback. We *believe* that we are seen by others as we see ourselves. We are supposed to be the authority figures in the home and on the job, and if we happen to meet a challenge to that point of view, our security is threatened.

The fastest way to find out if someone is listening is simply to ask. You can say, "Please repeat back to me what you heard me say." On the return side, to help others understand, you can say, "Now, what I heard you say was..." This is basic stuff, folks, but it is amazing how rarely it is used, and how effective it can be in communication. I recommend communication courses to my clients, but the truth is few of them have anything more profound than this to offer. We are so packaging-oriented in our culture that more often than not we think the fancy package gives the product value. This is a great tool for kids, because they are geniuses at selective non-listening. Once they are pinned down, and have to repeat the communication, it is difficult to get out of it. It is called completing the loop. The message goes from one party to the other, and must be fed back to the originator.

As children, we learn to tune out our parents; it is a natural phenomenon. We want to do what we want to do. As we grow we transfer that selective non-listening habit to everyone in our lives, particularly our spouses, because psychologically we identify them with our parental impressions. With men today the issue is particularly involved because it is so difficult for us to handle not having answers, or God forbid, that we should be wrong about an issue. The first, and I believe most important, issue is unconditional love for ourselves. To know that we can be wrong, that we don't have to know all the answers all the time and be OK about it is wonderful work. Humility works wonders with kids, and, by the way, does not go unnoticed by women. For the single or childless man, the work may well be with his own father. We all grow up with father hunger, and each of us must deal with it the way that best suits our natures. It must, however, be dealt with, if we are ever to be free men.

Imperatively, we must view our children in the light of unconditional love and communicate that our love for them is for a very special human being. Whatever they do or do not do should have no effect on how we feel about them. *Then all we have to do is live up to that standard.* Of course, in practical terms, we bring all of our own beliefs and patterning into each encounter we have. Many of these patterns manifest themselves in anger and frustration, and that is why to work on ourselves is so important. We are the last ones to see it, but the feedback is there. We need only to *look* and listen, statistically the two areas in which most women find men most lacking.

Kids need to see that their fathers, like themselves, are vulnerable, so that each can realize that we all make mistakes; that excellence is a far better goal than perfection; and that we don't always achieve our goals. By discussing such things as the father's digressions, the child begins to realize that mistakes are wonderful learning experiences, and it's OK to have some in one's history.

A good way to discuss vulnerabilities is in a group environment, such as Scouting, Indian Guides (YMCA,) Church camps, etc. Here an audience can help buffer the possible serious nature of such adventures. One such vehicle is a monthly "wilderness experience" tour, which I run in the Arizona mountains, where groups of six fathers and sons from all over the country spend five nights and six days looking at such things. Here, after a long day's hiking, we sit by a campfire and share our experiences in a light and supportive atmosphere. Fathers have the opportunity to share long-forgotten versions of their sons' behavior patterns, and get an opportunity to see them perhaps in a different light. As the sharing of these experiences extends throughout the group, the men, if they allow it to happen, begin to feel an opening up to the awareness of their vulnerabilities, touching feelings long repressed and events long denied. This opening up can be likened to a full cup of water. Once full, the cup will hold no more water. Any additional water added will merely spill over the edge. Fresh, new water can only be added if the cup is partially emptied first. Beliefs and attitudes collected during our lives quickly fill our emotional cups, and shared experiences act to empty them out and allow fresh, new ideas and possibilities to enter.

It has been my experience that we are all pretty much the same, and once we get beneath the surface imagery of what we want others to think we are, we react to outside stimuli much the same way as most others. In a wilderness environment, these similarities are emphasized because of the group dynamic - not unlike the camaraderie occurring under conditions of high stress such as hostage situations or natural disasters. We will talk more about the wilderness that exists in each of us. It is important for men to express the primal calls. We get to see ourselves through the unlimitedness of the wilderness rather than the limited parameters of society. The glass and concrete of the city are non-living matter. They absorb energy and give nothing back. Nature, on the other hand, inhales our presence and gives back new life.

Years ago I had a friend back in Pennsylvania. He told the story that whenever he had a problem, he would go to his Dad and tell him what was troubling him. The father would contemplate, and when he had something to share, he'd say "let's go to the tree." They would walk across the lawn and, standing in the shadow of a huge old Oak, each in ritual fashion would pee on the tree and the Father would say his piece. My friend had few other memories of his father, but this was so significant to him that without even realizing it he had started this tradition with his own four-year-old son. I wonder sometimes if bad bladders just ran in the family, or if there was really something to it. There is a lot more to finding the primal male within than just peeing on a tree in the woods. There is a primal contact with nature that men have let go of in the name of civilization, and we are all the losers. It can be found by exercising the emotional side of our being, that rests in the right hemisphere of the brain.

Whether done as a group experience such as my tours, or on an individual "man-to-man" weekend, sharing the beauty and power of nature can do more for bonding men than anything else I've ever encountered. We don't seem to have any problems with exposing our kids to these concepts in the scouting programs and in summer camps as youngsters, but generally these are peer experiences. We convince ourselves that it is for them, but mostly we are glad to be free of them for a while. These programs are fine, but just imagine the greater value to be had by doing it *with them*. In this way we make ourselves available to demonstrate that we care. It's nice to know that your parents love you. It becomes real when it is demonstrated. Nowhere is it written that we outgrow our need to communicate with our children and parents. Love knows no age limits. The need to be close to someone you love and to share your feelings with them never diminishes. Only our willingness to share seems to fade with time, and it doesn't have to be that way. Most kids with problems in relationships and/or drugs and alcohol, or any other anti-social activity, are reacting to some form of imbalance in their lives. Most imbalances are traceable to problems, or lacking, in the parental relationship. The truth, whether we admit it or not, is that most strong parental relationships foster strong sibling and parent/ sibling relationships. It requires the same sensitivity to the needs of others. A good relationship does not just occur naturally. Families occur naturally, relationships grow, and nothing can grow without nourishment.

Few can live within a family structure without picking up the subtle nuances, positive or negative, spoken or repressed, going on with everybody else. As a species, we do not like to celebrate or suffer alone. Kids need to know what's going on with their parents, in order to be able to figure out what's going on with themselves. Unconditional love is one of the most significant ideas of our time, with regard to potential for change. Unconditional love takes great openness and a willingness to risk **giving**, and the result is the most productive of all human emotions: compassion. Love, like everything else, is only a moment in time and space, but unlike anything else it can only move if it is given away. Love that does not move dies. Any restrictions or conditions added slows down or totally derails its movement.

If your children are abusing themselves in any way, (and all resistance and negative reactions are self-abusive), knowing that you love them regardless will give them a powerful tool to help in dealing with their problems. Consider that no one can solve another's problem. We can only offer tools for them to apply themselves. With unconditional love comes the knowledge that someone cares for us as individuals, just because we are who we are. This knowledge encourages the kind of strength that can help deal with any situation, in a positive and productive manner. Self-abuse can create these same qualities also, but on a synthetic and fleetingly temporary basis through the peer group. If our kids feel they have true unconditional love, the synthetic, peer group form will be less attractive as an option.

The same concepts follow with the other trials that kids go through. The funny thing is that these problems are only microcosms of the rest of the world's problems. These are the same problems we all deal with wherever we go, and this is why the father and son relationship is so vital to the survival of the planet. The game is the same; only the names change. Our children have been said to be our greatest gifts, and with the opportunity they give us to learn, that phrase can only be the greatest of understatements. Let us not forget that we are learning together. If we as men can accept our children as learning the lessons they need to learn and support them from an inner wealth of love and patience just because they are who they are, everything will work out just fine. We, as parents, will tell them anyway who and what we would like them to be, and there is great value in that, **but they will be who they will be, regardless of what we want.**

Understand the concept of unconditional love. Feel it. Make it a part of who you are, and most importantly, express it in action. You'll see relationships begin to develop in ways that you never thought possible. The next step will be to transfer that learning experience to the other relationships in your life, and the attraction of human abundance will have begun, not only for you, but for all those you touch. Unconditional love can be applied at any level of relationship, business, or activity. Think of it as merely respecting another person's right, need and desire to be all he/she can be, or not be. Allowing each to make his/her own choices.

How does one begin to experience this unconditional love? There is only one place to start, and that is with father. It is not necessary that your father be alive or present to create the experience. The exercise that follows will allow you a sense of what that experience can be. Choose a quiet place to read this, and just allow whatever comes up emotionally to do so. It is equally effective for men and women, if it is taken seriously. This kind of exercise can be done many times, and the more emotion it brings up the better.

EXERCISE #1

Remember, if you're a Mom or Dad, the hopes and dreams you had for your kid's as they lay in the cradle - if you're a young man or woman, see in your mind the love and expectations your parents had as you lay there, helpless, dependent and totally vulnerable. **Children** are the most precious gift the universe has to offer. Without them there is no tomorrow, today or yesterday. Somehow or another, as the years go by, we get caught up in our lives and something happens...the intense love that we feel in those tender moments in the cradle gets diluted with life and life's processes. It doesn't lessen it, it doesn't die, it just gets spread out over a complex and confusing life. So many things and so many people demand our attention, our time, our emotions. We tire, from being pulled in many directions...I'd like to talk a bit about Fathers...there is one of us, very near to each of us. We come in every conceivable size, shape and color. Mostly we exist in the background. Mom was the one who tied our shoes, healed our wounds and wiped away the tears. Dad went to work. Oh, he was usually there when we really needed him...he paid the taxes, he painted the gutters, and drove the car when the family went shopping. The one time when most of us could be sure he was around was when the punishment needed to be dealt out. But, even if he never said so, we knew he loved us; and he did...or he does. For some of us he was even less visible...maybe for others not visible at all. Perhaps for you as it was for me, he is mostly an image...a composite of all our heroes, off on a secret mission, to return someday with wonderful gifts and stories of great adventures. A dream never realized. Perhaps he really wasn't very nice sometimes. Perhaps he had his own problems, which made him angry or distant and we just didn't understand in our innocence. But deep down we knew he loved us; and he did or he does. What's vital for us to know now as we grow older, and follow our heritage (which is the only path to fatherhood that we know), is that whatever you or he did or did not do was the only thing you or he could have done, in that time and in that place. If he could have done differently, he surely would have. For the truth about life is that we are, in each moment, perfection. We do that which we do because it is the perfect thing for us to do given the space we are in, and the lessons we have to teach and to learn. History and others' opinions may take a different point of view about his actions, but right and wrong have no place in the moment in which we live. The concept of right and wrong separates us from the perfection that we are, and puts us into judgment of ourselves and others. Yes, we do what we do, because the only other choice we have is to do nothing. And as long we breathe the beauty of life, we simply cannot do nothing. We take the actions that we need to take, and learn the lessons that we need to learn. There is no inherent rightness or wrongness about any action, there are only our judgments about them. Judgments are beliefs that we hold as truth. Truth is everyman's and everyman's truth is different. What is important to do now is to get in touch with our feelings about fatherness. About forgiving our fathers for not living up to our expectations, and forgiving ourselves for not living up to theirs. It is called the impossible dream. And in the process we'll get to look at our feelings about ourselves, our masculine and feminine relationships, the whole of our being.

Now, let's take a little trip, and hold for a moment, the gift that it brings for us. Take one or two deep breaths and form a picture in your mind of a warm, old house with rich wood paneling, soft dark carpets and wide, gently winding staircases. Let's go up one of those sets of stairs into an attic, full of memories and dreams of childhood. Over in one corner find an old trunk that holds all the promises of yesterday, open the top and look in. Under the old blankets you'll find a photo album... imagine yourself reaching in...take it out and blow off the dust...open to the first page...there is a picture of you, sitting in a room with a two-year-old boy. Just for now, let's say that you are the father and the boy is your son. It's a warm spring day, and he's dressed in a little white T shirt and rubber training pants. You're doing whatever it is that you are doing, and he's rummaging around in a cardboard box full of his stuff. You stop and watch him, so hard at play. He is so totally involved in his moment that he doesn't notice you're watching. His little truck is as real and big to him as he moves it along the floor as any truck will ever be. Then, suddenly he sees a ball, and instantly, the truck is forgotten, and the ball becomes the only thing in his life. As he gets up and chases it around the room, his little legs and feet are seemingly disconnected from his body. Without warning, he plows at full speed into the side of a lamp table and falls with a well-padded thud to the carpeted floor, unbroken but so suddenly jolted back to his other reality, that he begins to cry and reaches out in your direction. What is your reaction? Do you go to his truth in that moment that he hurts and hug him gently with soft, loving words and positive reinforcement? Do you scold him for running wildly in the house, when, after all, you've told him so many times not to? Do you disregard it? Do you call for someone else to handle it? Know that whatever you did was absolutely the best thing for you to do in your moment, or you would not have done it. Based on where and who you were at that moment in time, you made the only choice you could have made. How did he react to your choice? What lasting emotional reinforcement was created in him by the interaction? How descriptive is this scenario of your overall relationship with him? How are you and he playing that same game today, five or ten or fifteen years later, or perhaps twenty or thirty years later? What's been lost, and what's been saved, in the years that flew by so quickly, while you were busy building your career, or planning for your retirement? Now, go back into your album. Turn back to some older, dustier pages. Now it's thirty or more years earlier. Now, the scene is the same, but the players are you and your father. What similarities are there? What results do you see? How do you feel about what's going in that room? Just spend a moment here and feel the emotion as it comes up for you. Come back slowly through the years, experiencing whatever comes up for you to the moment of now, and project forward fifteen years into the future. Once again, the scene is the same, but this time the players are your son and your grandson. What does the moment of their reality look like, and what are the gifts they are sharing? What changes occurred, or did not occur, between the passing generations that made the interaction different?...or was there any change at all...are you still seeing the same results?

Certainly there is nothing you can do to change that which has gone before, but what *can* you do to change the future? Whom can you love enough to make the difference...the answer is really quite simple...the one constant through all the generations-*you*. It is sad but true: we cannot share that which we do not have, and self-love is the greatest possible gift we have to share. Self-love can only be unconditional, so what better place to start?

COMMITMENT
Until one is committed
there is hesitancy, the chance to draw back,
always ineffectiveness.
Concerning all acts of initiative (and creation)
there is one elementary truth,
the ignorance of which kills countless ideas
and splendid plans:
that the moment one definitely commits oneself,
then Providence moves too.
All sorts of things occur to help one
that would otherwise never have occurred.
A whole stream of events issues from the decision,
raising in one's favor all manner
of unforseen incidents and meetings
and material assistance,
which no man could have dreamt
would have come his way.

W.N. Murray, The Scottish Himalayan Expedition - 1951

TOOL# 3
The Structure of Relationship

Gifts often come in unmarked packages. The greatest gift I ever received is the first I'll share with you. *The gift is the view of the relationship being an independent and separate reality, greater than the components of which it is made up.* As a result, a relationship creates its own needs and requires its own nourishment. It is sometimes necessary to look at being involved with another person as being involved with three separate entities; yourself, that person, and the relationship itself. A concept that has worked well with me in dealing with my own boys is thinking of them as having chosen their parents, with us having had nothing to do with it. They, knowing on a soul level, the lessons needed to be learned, seeing that we would allow them the conditions in which to learn them. These may be negative conditions as well as positive ones. These "visualizations" create an atmosphere in which we must constantly be looking at what the lessons are, both for them and ourselves. Often this exploration process becomes the path of understanding.

When my son got into drugs is when I became aware of my own relationship problems. I "believed" that he was developing just fine, while I ran my life and built a business. I became aware that he needed to get my attention. He achieved this through a series of self-abusive tactics that ranged from drugs to grand theft, over an eighteen-month period. In absolute desperation, I packed him into the car and drove him to the police station, where I asked the juvenile intake officer to make him a ward of the court. I was at my wits' end, and was as angry as he was. My fear quite frankly was that I would physically abuse him, and I loved him too much to allow that to happen.

(What I did not realize until much later was that the anger and fear were all mine, projected onto him. He was merely mirroring it back to me in the only way he could.) The juvenile system in Fairfax County, Virginia, where we lived at the time, may be one of the best in the country, but that does not allow them the luxury to fill everyone's needs. Like most, they were over-crowded and not able to handle situations that were not critical from the legal point of view. When I took him in we were escorted to a small office, myself, my son and my wife, who like me had just given up in utter frustration. When the officer came in, all my negative belief systems were brought into full focus for me to deal with. On one hand I had terrible guilt about not being able to handle this. All my weakness and feelings of not being enough came up. At the same time I was asking the court system, in front of my wife and the world, to take my own child away from me because I was a failure as a parent

But the real test came as the officer, a black woman in her early twenties, sat down to handle this for us.

We talked, and told our stories, and she just listened. She was unable, or thank God, unwilling to consider taking him from the family structure. She suggested that we write up a legal contract, which would define the expectations of both him as a son, and my wife and me as parents. *What I saw was that we had never communicated with each other on a level that allowed us to understand what the parent/child relationship was all about.* We had gone through all those years of setting and breaking rules and regulations, but never defining the game. We left the courthouse and after about three days of negotiation, we came to an uneasy agreement of acceptable behavior for all of us. No one got what he wanted, but each of us got some defined parameters within which we could start building a relationship that showed promises that it could work.

There are no immediate solutions; in fact, it took about a year to begin seeing results, but we stayed with it. It also changed the way I looked at my life, because I realized that we all do the same thing with most of the people in our lives. For me the "contract" became a symbol of success in relationships. In fact, it became the essence of the relationship. Whenever we get out of agreement with the contract, we have someplace to go to either re-establish intent or renegotiate our expectations. I have found this to be an incredibly important tool in improving peoples lives. Somewhere in Virginia is a wonderful lady, a black social worker, who has been a catalyst for change in some very important lives. I thank her for that, and only hope she knows the good she has done.

We live in an age in which many find it very easy to devalue relationships purely on the basis of immediate gratification. That gratification can be social, sexual, financial or security based. We move from relationship to relationship *as though the inner peace and substance of who we are could be found in another person.* A challenge...Ponder the following idea: You already have, by definition of your existence, everything you need to live your life in abundance and joy! *It is all in the process of thought.* Our conscious mind creates images (thoughts) from choice. Negative, positive, good, bad, active, passive, all choices that create our conscious thought patterns. As we have noted, the unconscious mind is where all of our automatic operation and reaction are created. So once again we see that through the conscious mind input, we have absolute control of who we are and what we want to be. By allowing ourselves the right to consciously surround ourselves with positive, joyful experiences, the subconscious learns to react in a like manner. It is called manifesting our own reality. The conscious mind makes the choices about what we eat, the subconscious merely has the responsibility to digest and assimilate what we give it. If we eat foods that make us ill, create disease and make us overweight, that is our conscious choice. It has nothing to do with inherent subconscious desire until we form those habits within it. Much of what we call awareness or potentials training is based on this subconscious reprogramming.

According to Dr. Frederick Bailes, one of the founders of the Science of Mind Church, eventually all man's thoughts appear in some form in his life. It is widely held that the brain records and stores somewhere within its depths literally 100 percent of everything we see, hear or experience, whether we are aware of it or not. It follows then that much of how we react is not created from our conscious desire but from unconscious reaction. This constitutes the law of cause and effect as it relates to human experience. *We are the cause of all of our effects.*

The universal laws of human interaction say that we draw into relationships those people from whom we can learn as well as teach. The relationships occur as a result of the student-teacher interaction. If no learning occurs then no relationship develops. Often that learning opportunity can be difficult to spot. In fact, if we live our lives without consciously looking for what we can learn, the chances are good we will never see them. The process is called mirroring. If we look around, for instance, and notice that we are surrounded by heavily negative people, the chances are that we are also in a negative state at that moment. The subconscious will convince us that "that's the way people are," and makes it OK to be negative. From Neuro-Linguistic Programming, the study of communication on the human response system, comes the observation that *"The meaning of the message is the response that it elicits."* - The communication that we get back is a direct result of the communication that we put out- We are 100 percent responsible for our relationships, through our communication. The learning opportunity comes from introducing positive possibilities to the conscious awareness, so reprogramming, or repatterning as it is called, can occur. The mystical part of this interaction is called love. Parental relationships break up, usually because the love, (sometimes misspelled "passion"), deteriorates for any one of a thousand reasons. (We can find as many reasons as we need.) The result statistically is that two people split, to repeat the same experience with someone else, with similar results and disappointments. This without ever looking at the relationship as a separate entity, and defining what "relationship" means, through a contract of understanding. The three-part relationship contract works with anyone and everyone, and helps to prevent falling into neediness, which convinces us that we somehow are incomplete without that other person. We really don't need anyone else to complete us, and even if we did, and could find her or him, it is an unreasonable expectation to put on anyone else. Besides, they are having the same difficulties finding the solutions to their problems as we are.

If the option of looking at relationships as a separate entity is allowed, we might discover some interesting things. Such as: *a new point of view about our partner's right to differ with us; How our ability to learn and grow is enhanced by sublimating our desires to new possibilities; That commitment creates movement.* We then can apply these lessons, not only to our own happiness with our partners, but in supporting a much higher level of security in our kids, allowing them more opportunity for love and responsibility. What is more important is that they take it into their lives as they grow, improve upon it and, with God's help, perhaps we *can* save the world.

I am not proposing that all relationships are, or even should be, sacred, in an operational sense, or that we do not make mistakes in choosing partners or that all parent/child conflicts are perfectly solvable. What I am suggesting is that a relationship can exist either negatively or positively in or out of the formal partnership. As adults and parents it is our choice. If the mated partners can learn to take positive responsibility and stay out of guilt, blame and victim positions, the kids will emulate it and do the same in their relationships. They can *see* that it works by demonstration. It is what their conscious mind experiences that becomes the basis for their subconscious and unconscious responses.

...and the trouble is,
if you don't risk anything
you risk even more.

Erica Jong

TOOL# 4
RISK and FEAR

Earlier I mentioned that unconditional love was a risk, perhaps for many men and women the biggest risk of their lives. We need to look at risk and see it for what it really is, and more importantly, what it is not. Consider another possibility; *That we are all mirror images of one another, and we see in others that which we see in ourselves, both negatively and positively.* Let's start this chapter off with a *real* risk. Looking at who we are. Consider the following statement as true for a moment, regardless of your resistance to it: "If you want to find out who you are, look carefully at your friends." We attract those who will support us in our belief systems and reject those who do not. An honest look can tell us much. One of the reasons that the list of attributes for men over forty (page 29) is so dismal, is that most men cannot handle finding out who they are and fear association with others will make them look at it. They are not up for the risk.

If you don't have friends but do have kids, look at them; the same is true. If you have more than one child of the same sex, your experience might well be the same as mine. Each is probably totally different in nature and personality types, and yet you are fully represented in each of them. If you have lived with them for the majority of their lives, this is more likely true whether they are your natural children or not. How can they be so different, and yet each be so much like you **and** their mother? My oldest boy is a "walking party"; shorter than I, physically stronger, athletic, extroverted, impetuous, and far more gregarious. What one would call a pure "promoter" or type A personality. My other son is taller than I, non-athletic, lean, introverted, creative, musical, and very detail-oriented. A typical "analyst" type. Yet, as different as each of them is, I can look at each of them and find it difficult to see where I end and they begin. It is true on an emotional level as well as a physical level. During their early years, I was busy building a career and following what was at that time my image of what a father was supposed to be. What it took me years to discover was that the image was primarily that of a token diaper changer. But that is all I knew. I can see now how my own impatience, authority issues, and belief systems shaped and formed them. They were just mirroring back to me what I gave them in my communication. I carry more guilt about the bad things than I need to, but am working on it, and have much pride about the good. I love the good in each of us and merely accept the bad as part of the growth each of us required. It gives us lots to work on. This is not an easy growth each of us required. It gives us lots to work on. This is not an easy place to get to, of course. *It takes commitment and willingness to take responsibility.*

As I matured and realized that there was more to life than material acquisition, I began looking for ways to relate to my boys. *The process of getting in touch with them allowed me to get in touch with myself.* That process and its importance to men and women in cleaning up the relationship quagmire is the vital message of our times. My whole world changed *from a perceptive point of view.* What I mean by that is, nothing out there changed at all, until *I* began to look at things from a different perspective. I realized the reason my boys were so different and yet so much like me, was simply because all human beings share the same basic attributes. We can be only so many things, and we can go about being who we are in just so many ways. We constantly change and adapt to our changing environment, but we all use the same basic tools. Once I changed my view of the world and took some responsibility for that view, the world suddenly started to act the way I had always wanted it to. All the people in my life started reacting differently and responding to me in a far more positive way. Changing my viewpoint of the world represented to me an enormous risk, but the results would have been worth it even if the risk had been real, rather than all in my mind.

No discussion of risk can be complete, without a look at its co-conspirator, fear. One comes up automatically with the other, and the quality of the risk is inherent in the amount of fear created within. *"Fear,"* some wise ancient sage once said, *"is a fight we have with our own reflection."* This is perhaps the only way it could be, because as we are responsible for creating our fears, so are we responsible for what we do with them.

Outside events may have given us the opportunity to react, but we choose the fear, out of many options available to us. Fear can be handled in many ways. We can give our fears power over us, make them an ally, ignore them, stuff them, or use them as a learning experience. Often in relationships, risk comes with fear in the form of powerlessness. We view our ability to seek solutions to our problems negatively, because we fear what might happen if they are insolvable, or that we might lose the relationship. The ego tells us that a lousy relationship is better than none at all. We then withdraw into what I will call our comfort zones, powerless, never attempting to find out if we could have solved them or not. Our inaction empowers the fear and the fear gets the power, not us. And nothing happens to correct the problem, but much *can* happen to make it worse. Fear is resistance to dealing with the moment.

Resistance closes down our awareness, creating more fear. Fear is an emotional closing down process, a withdrawing from our reality. Withdrawal is a contraction of energy, a sink hole in the universe, that results in anger, pain, ignorance and hatred. Not an easy way to cause fun relationships! Zen teaches us that there are only two innate fears: that of loud noises, and that of falling. All the rest are learned responses. Emerson perhaps said it best in observing, *"What torments of grief you endured for evils which never arrived."* How much of our lives are spent avoiding the *fear* of failure? Failure is merely another new opportunity for us to seek success, and in that way serves us positively.

Fear can be best used as a teacher. When you feel fearful of approaching someone on any subject, know that you can only learn and grow by moving into the fear. The only way around fear is through it! Don't let the fear of hurting someone stand in the way of telling them what they need to hear. Don't let the fear of losing a relationship stand in the way of saving it.

Earlier in this chapter I discussed how my own personal growth began. What was happening was that I was learning how to love. Putting love out into my world and getting it back! When we look into a mirror, we see exactly what we are. We may or may not like what we see, but that's what is there. Every pair of eyes out there is no more than a mirror reflecting back who we are. To love that pair of eyes is to love oneself. If we find fault, judgment and prejudice in the eyes of others, it's reflecting back on us. The risk comes in being willing to accept that what we see *is* us. Once that can be achieved, we can set about changing the reflection, but not until then. As a man, learning to love has been my single greatest accomplishment in life.

What I did was take the biggest risk of my life. I went outside my "comfort zone." The term "comfort zone" describes that area in which we allow ourselves to operate in our daily lives; an area that represents no risk to our comfort level. (Comfort has no relationship to what's good for us.) I began doing trainings and seminars that showed me how to expand beyond the artificial barriers of my beliefs. These efforts were a substantial risk, from both financial and time considerations, as well as a challenge to all my comfort levels. But risk is just another component of growth, and without growth we die inside and the legacy we leave is a very boring one. I have my own judgment about being boring. Some folks may like it.

To look at our kids and say "I love you, just because you are who you are," takes a huge commitment to risk. To say that one must also know and admit that you love who *you* are. Once willing and able to take that risk, the rewards are also huge.

In addition, the ability to commit to risk in other areas of your life will increase dramatically. Our kids, physically, emotionally and spiritually are only extensions of ourselves, yet totally self-contained and unique within themselves. Our belief systems and expectations of them create relationship blocks. Once we take the risk to be responsible for our relationships, we find that the responsibility will be shared by others. What is learned will be transferred to all relationships. If only one thousand people read this book and positively affect two other people in their lives, it won't take very long for the reverse domino theory to take hold and change the world. There can be no argument with the reality of what one person can do to change the world.

We can find many examples in history of those whose impact has been indelible, through sheer commitment to purpose. Hold humbly but not lightly your power to cause change. I certainly do not want my kids or grandkids to die the abysmal deaths of nuclear fallout or starvation because of no drinkable water, or create mutations of themselves through ingestion of non-biodegradable poisons. (I seriously doubt that you want that either.) Take a good look at the potential that risk carries for good, weighed against the risk of no risk. As in everything we do in life, we are in a position of choice to act or not. If you see that you are a victim of circumstance and are convinced you can't change anything, take a small risk and just consider how your life and the lives of those you love might change if you were willing to take a bigger risk. If you are intrigued by the possibilities, do a wilderness journey with your son or your father, a potentials training, or just take a walk with him in the woods. Listen to your heart, and if it works for you, pee on a tree together.

It sometimes is easier to understand a concept when we break it down into easily recognizable symbology. We can do that with the terms Risk and Fear, in the following manner:

R ejecting
I nsecurity to
S eek
K nowledge

F alse
E vidence
A ppearing
R eal

68

Think about these terms, and their implications in regard to your life and how your belief systems control your actions. On balance, conquering fear by using risk to gain awareness, is the real growth process. There is, of course, a hook. There are two kinds of risk; responsible, or positive risk, and its obvious opposite. We will discuss only positive risk because it is consistent with our process.

POSITIVE RISK

First a little morsel of wisdom I can't resist, and in fact run my life by: *Nothing happens without commitment.* No growth, no forward movement of any kind can occur until we make a commitment to make it happen. Problem relationships will remain problems until a decision is made to do something about them. *Making no decision is a forfeiture*; in effect, a commitment to make a relationship not work. How many of us have spent fruitless, frustrating years in relationships that didn't work while doing nothing about them? Perhaps we find some reward in suffering, that being a rationalization of our guilt (well-deserved punishment), for doing nothing to make the relationship better. The result is we beat ourselves up, on a subconscious level, for not having the guts to either get out of it, or take responsibility for making it work. Very few relationships can survive ten or twenty years without going through at least one period of physical or emotional separation, and usually several.

Again, it comes down to choices. We often end up in marriage or family counseling sessions, spending hard-earned money to try to find out what we already know, and apply solutions that we already have within us. I do not have a prejudice against this type of counseling, but it is an example of how readily we are willing to go outside ourselves to find answers to our problems, rather than sit down and develop communication lines that work. What is required is a commitment to ourselves and each other to be honest, and explore the problems and the options. By considering the relationship as a separate entity it is possible to view all the problems in a different light. The risk is that we might find ways to work out the problems. Often just discussing the options can provide the partners with a point of view that can open up desires to correct divergent paths.

Most couples who have been together for many years have a history of relationship with much value that is easy to overlook in the heat of conflict.

relationship with much value that is easy to overlook in the heat of conflict. We tend to want to look outside our immediate experience to find that which we are not willing to believe already exists. Non-acceptance of the positive aspects of our relationships is a major reason we blame our partners for the problems. Without accepting our own responsibility, for both the good and the bad, our relationships will continue to falter. It may be hard to accept for some, but the truth is that if one-half of a relationship is not working, neither is the other.

Creating positive risk is looking at a situation that appears hopeless, and finding a way to make it work. Most relationships that fail, fail for the wrong reasons, and the parties involved rarely understand why. The really unfortunate part is that the lessons are never learned. The chances of any subsequent relationships working can be no better, if we do not learn our lessons initially. The lesson is commitment.

Commitment is a peculiar kind of highly creative energy source, perhaps the most highly creative. Once a commitment is made, amazing things happen to support the commitment. There is no magic in it, just our senses opening up to be able to see things that have always been there but which we missed for one reason or another. Making a commitment is another process of emptying the cup discussed in an earlier chapter. One needs to find quiet time in a special place, to get to the bottom of what it is that we want to create in our relationships. Those of the "new age" call it "manifestation," but it's really only that super powerful inner knowing, committing to do want *you* want done. "Fixing" relationships is, of course, not a simple matter. and just committing alone will accomplish nothing. I am not even sure that a relationship can be "fixed." Rather we learn to adjust our reactions and casualness to work in harmony with others. Committing to doing *something* is positive risk. A willingness is required to step out of our comfort zones long enough to risk rejection and failure, so that we may discover these feelings exist only as concepts we create.

There is a very simple process for demonstrating this principle in your own life. Find a person with whom you have developed a non - or negative relationship by choice. Preferably no one close or important to you. Someone who embodies a number of your prejudices. Commit to being with that person long enough to get to know a little about them. Something as simple as sharing a few minutes over a cup of coffee. Several things will happen; you'll get to see the connection between risk and fear; you'll get to feel how resistance controls our lives; you'll get to see how our beliefs about how we think things are limits our participation in our lives; you might make a friend; and you might in the process teach the same lessons to that other person. A simple illustration? Yes. But if you look carefully there will be representations of both you and your son in that other person.

The difference between us, equal the likenesses. It's called Universal balance.

REJECTION

Without exception the one overriding concern of almost every one in this society appears to be the fear of rejection. It is so dominant that when people are asked in groups to state their greatest fears, whatever comes in second generally gets lost in the discussion. Why is it that we are so afraid of being rejected? Some of it goes back to the breaking of the bonding between mother and child. This is particularly critical with boys, because as we have seen generally there is no father to turn to for emulation. Perhaps out of their own personal guilt, many psychologists have supported the idea of quality time being more important than quantity time. I suggest that this is an attempt to fit a round solution to a square problem rather than solving the problem. It reminds me of contemporary politics, in which giving half the people half of what they need, to avoid offending anyone, is considered a job well done. Nothing can replace time, good or bad, spent with our children. For girls, the bonding with mother lasts much longer and the ties are far stronger. They too, however, get strong implants of rejection from the non-present father. In truth we never lose our mothers, sometimes to our detriment, but we rarely find our fathers until late in our lives. But he always comes up.

Being rejected brings up those memories of being left alone a child, or with a strange babysitter, or perhaps the first day of school. Uncomfortable and often sad feelings, all based in insecurity. The reason we do not want to be rejected is that we do not believe that we are strong enough or good enough to survive all by ourselves. For men this fear is heavily father dominated because we haven't had the continuous role modeling to provide us with the strength we need to believe we are enough. There are no shortcuts around this problem. It takes work to get through these blockages, and that starts with simply accepting the fact that it may be so. Believing that rejection is important makes it so. Believing that we may be rejected in a given situation creates a limitation for us at that moment, and belief in limits creates limited people.

We carry our experiences as children into our lives in every moment. As you think about this, think about how your children are absorbing your life and know that they will take that with them also. Every time they are rejected, another filter is layered on, to convince them that they are rejectable. The transference is to the outside and the inference is that others have the ability to reject us. Looking closely at this belief we can see that this is literally impossible. Rejection comes from within ourselves. We allow ourselves to be rejected by believing that it can be done. If we can learn to override the old programming, rejection can become a thing of the past, and we won't bring it into our relationships and our kids won't learn to fear it.

A second cause of the fear of rejection may well be the process of expectation. Expectation is a judgment we put on others as a result of how we believe they should behave. It is our picture that determines the outcome of another's response. We are interpreting that response through our filters, and the room for error is immense. Generally our fear in a situation gets in our way of handling it, and then the fear becomes self-fulfilling. This is why understanding the process of the belief system is so important. But it is also important to note that the understanding is only the beginning. Life is not about understanding, it's about being. The understanding is a left-brained process through which we must travel to get to "being," which is only a another phrase for "living in the moment." Once we get to that place of "being," security and inner peace abound and rejection heads for the museum. Once we've dealt with rejection, fear can't be far behind.

*When you have to make a choice
and don't make it, that is in
itself a choice.*

William James

TOOL #5
VISUALIZATION/AFFIRMATION

As we look at the tools for personal improvement, one factor is readily noticeable. They are all tied in together, each dependent on the others for wholeness. The art of visualization has been exercised for centuries in many forms. The term derives from "vision," or "dream," to make real in the mind the unknown. It is a vital part of manifestation, or creating in material form that which we desire to have. The process involves repatterning of the sub/unconscious mind to allow us to accept new realities. In relationships we must learn to visualize ourselves with others in the way we wish it to be. By so doing the brain finds a way of recognizing opportunities to create. This is a process of universal energy in motion. The energy of which we are made needs only to be directed by the mind. Every course of self-improvement I have ever seen is based on this simple law. Applied to the relationship, it is done by a mental picture of what you want and with whom. That puts the commitment in visible form. The factor of responsibility comes in listening and evaluating the feedback, and adjusting our belief systems to allow the vision to be completed by the universal flow.

I choose to view the universe as the ultimate work of art with all aspects of it in constant flow around a balance point. Expansion in one part creates a compensating contraction in another. The energy that flows through the universe also flows in corresponding paths from the macro-universe down through successive levels to the micro-universe of the single-celled organism. All things are related through some form of energy and flow around a balance point. We as humans, have a balance of this energy that we call masculine and feminine. Science generally agrees that at the point of conception we are truly androgenous, or without sexual definition. Through our early development we become a mixture of male and female, with one dominating the other. We do not, however, lose the influences of the other gender. This specific energy spoken of is not necessarily genetic sexuality, but energy of the psyche, manifested through the ego. How we think and operate with regard to our egos is a result of this energy balance, but not part of it. The recognition of the balance between these feminine and masculine energies in each individual, in each relationship, in each society, will be critical in determining the quality of our experience of the final years of this century.

Contemporary American society is very much "results oriented" and places its highest values on those results, rather than the processes that create them. We are all familiar with the saying "the results justify the means." This, in my opinion, has been one of the most damaging concepts to the balance of masculine energy ever penned. What women seem to know intuitively men seem to have great trouble handling. "It's not what you do, it's how you do it"; "It's not what you say, it's how you say it," are concepts not readily understood by many men. The "what" is the masculine, active result. The "how" is the feminine, feeling process. Studies in body language and Neuro-Linguistic Programming (NLP) show that we have become masters at camouflaging what we mean by what we say, and it is because we are out of balance in how we "think" vs. how we "feel." In fact it is estimated through NLP studies that only 10 to 15 percent of our communication is through our spoken vocabulary. The rest come from subconscious physical messages through body movements, voice tone, volume rhythm and many other signals, which are controlled by the right brain. Thinking is a mind process, but feeling is a heart process. Both are natural, and instinctive reactions, both require constant development. The basis of this whole 20th Century revolution is feeling. Getting in touch with feelings that will not necessarily change what we already believe to be true, but will allow us additional sources of intuitive input upon which we can make choices.

Our "maleness" images have been based on results for so long that when we are faced with lack of results such as losing a war, a job, failed relationships, etc. we go to pieces. We blame communism, the boss, drugs in schools, pornography, the women's rights movement, ad infinitum, to avoid looking at the process which brought us our results. *In truth, we each have in our lives what we want, at any given moment.* That is a pretty powerful statement, and I will explain it as follows.

Our conscious mind is the sensory depository of all outside stimuli. This is the collection point from which all our choices are made. The result of this process of choice is called thought. As we discussed earlier, these thoughts pass into, and become part of, our subconscious, making up our automatic response system. Belief systems, prejudices, preferences and blockages we experience in our daily lives are the demonstration of our automatic response system. *So our thoughts then, create, or manifest, our reality, and manifestation is the DNA of the Universe.* Our reality is what we have. We have what we have because we visualized it, and if we visualized it, we must have wanted it! To change it one needs to make new choices and create new automatic response systems. If we truly didn't want what we've got, we would not have created it. That is how we set up our lessons. This whole process is neither inherently good nor bad, it is just the way the mind works. The subconscious mind is our true computer. In its healthy state it cannot make choices, but can only respond to its programming. Again it is vital that we view the conscious mind as the place where our choices, and therefore our results, are manifested. Our live experience can be nothing less than a demonstration of our thoughts. If your relationship with anyone in your life is not what it could be, try acknowledging that it is because your conscious thought processes have created that. Then make conscious affirmative statements about how you want the relationship to be.

Although visualization has been a respectable tool for centuries, affirmations have been given a bad rap in recent years because many feel that by simply saying over and over twenty times a day that you desire something to be so, it will happen. Actually, an affirmation is only a verbalized visualization. The value of affirmations is that it opens the left brain's natural resistance to new action through auto suggestion. It literally puts our resistance into a temporary trance state from which the right brain can go to work generating positive *action* to create. But we must be fully co-creative in the process, or we merely become blind mediators. I like to think of a goal as just a dream with a deadline. Once the goal is clear, the questions about how to attain the goal will appear. This is the point where outside guidance ceases to be effective except as a crutch. Only you have the answers that will work for you. This is the process where the lessons of life are learned on the spiritual level. We visualize our desires through the Godself within and tap into it through the right brain.

By actively seeking answers from within, the emphasis changes from results to process. For example, in a situation where a teen wants to get concert tickets that go on sale during a school day, it might look something like this: *results:* "OK stupid, why'd you cut class and get suspended from school?" to *process:* "OK son, how are you going to handle getting tickets for the rock concert *and* keep your commitment to school?" Your attention to his needs by being involved with him *before* he reacts, in a way that teaches him how to balance his wants with his responsibilities, can avoid stressful confrontation in all facets of the relationship. Not being expelled from school will change the nature of the conflict between you and him, and those each of you touch. The positive reaction developed in a good working relationship cannot help but spill over to other people.

In the example above, the interaction involved has created what could be looked at as a circle of energy. The circle concept allows us a visual understanding of the continuing cyclical nature of things that can easily be absorbed by the conscious mind; by visualizing energy in a constant, never ending flow, moving from the earth plane into the universe, being recharged and then recycled back to earth. Through approaching our relationships with the circle concept in mind, we can give urselves the opportunity always to be aware that whatever we create in the moment we are in carries over to the next, and is amplified in its energy content. With this process we can get an idea of how powerful we truly are, in our ability to create. We can apply the concept to our daily lives by visualizing our relationships the way we would like them to be. But the trick is to visualize not only our view of it, but the whole relationship as a separate and integral unit. That way you will be forced to see both sides of the problem in the relationship. By "seeing" in the mind's eye all of your life's involvements, both positive and negative, as cyclical in energy content, you will never loose track of how powerful thoughts are.

Visualization and affirmation are concepts that work. A tool that can be applied to help get from where we are to where we would like to be. It is not a tool to avoid reality, but one to help us understand that we can have reality be whatever we want it to be. This is obviously a symbolic exercise in self motivation, a game, if you will, that we play with our minds. But it works! The results attainable through visualization can be remarkable. If you can grasp the concept, you will find that your relationships are already improving, just through your awareness. If we are to meet the growth challenges of the future, we must become far more interested in the process of how we handle ourlives, than in the results. If the process is a good one, so will be the results. A great lover is not one who climaxes every opportunity he gets with great gusto, but one who shares in the process of making love, and creates a condition in which loving becomes a separate entity which can be shared by both partners. The resulting experience has an energy greater than the sum of its parts. (Sound familiar?) It is just another example of living in the moment.

The next time you find yourself walking down a busy city street, try a little visualization. Pretend it's the year 1700 and you're the first white man to walk this land. You're the discoverer of this lush, virgin forest. Give yourself a neat name like "Ponce de Camino Real" or something. Enjoy the moment of fantasy (but watch the traffic lights). Feel the warm sunlight, inhale the fresh, dew-laden pure air. See young deer peeking at you through the dense underbrush, with a loving, unprejudiced interest. Enjoy the freedom of the moment. Then when you come back to what you perceive as reality, notice the lightness. Also notice you'll probably be smiling. Remember the joy of childhood daydreaming. I lost my own well-developed art of daydreaming as a result of spending many of my early school years doing it, much to the distress of my teachers. It took a concentrated effort as an adult to relearn it and know that it was not "wrong." It has, in fact, often been my salvation. In times of depression and end-of-the-ropelessness, knowing that I can create my own way out by just thinking it though a visualization, is my prayer to the God within. Through visualizations we can see our own potentials as limitless through the right brain, and experience the possible through the left. Once we experience our own vastness, we find ourselves suddenly falling in love with ourselves and our experience of life. The most amazing part is that the cycle continues reinforcing itself. Your son's self-image is based largely on his experience of you. Like it or not, that's usually the way it is, balanced with his fantasies and life experience. Effects of trauma, which can have powerful negative effects on personality development, are directly related to how you, the parent, related and handled the situation, and the child's perception of it. As youth of the power-filled years of the mid nineteen hundreds, our self-image has been exposed to great potential damage. We must be aware of its effect on our sons. It has been my general observation that due to broadly expanded communications, better education, greater exposure and increased general awareness, our kids are in better emotional shape generally than their parents. This is particularly true when one considers the importance of the choices being made. The truth about parent/child relationships is that we have as much to learn from them as they have from us. That's a pretty wonderful balance. Role modeling should not stop being a factor in any human experience, *and nowhere is it written in stone that the older must be the model, all of the time!*

The world does not wait for us to think about seriously examining our lives. The time has come to consciously take charge of our own futures. There is help out there, and all we need to do is ask. Enroll in a self help course or awareness training, or weekend seminar on some aspect of relationship. Join or create a men's or women's issues group with your friends to discuss areas of common interest. Getting started is the most difficult part, because we tend to look at these experiences as "fixing" something that is wrong, rather than an opportunity to expand. No one alive, regardless of the level of accomplishment, cannot expand and grow. Create direction, and the direction will create movement; movement creates growth; growth brings peace. In choosing courses or opportunities in which you might wish to become involved, keep in mind that no single approach can have all the answers. In fact, the only one who has any answers at all is you. Do not go outside yourself for anything other than available options. The more options exposed, the better the potential for quality choices. The only way any self awareness training, or books on self-help, or even professional counseling, can serve is to give a framework of support. Within that framework, you can compare your beliefs and attitudes with others who are equally concerned about their lives. We need to realize that we create our own reality, totally independent of anyone else, and we base that creative power on what we want, or on what we believe we want.

Visualiztion can be practiced, and it helps to practice by working with a subject that is meaningful to providing growth in those areas in which you desire expansion and understanding. It is nice to see oneself with several beautiful women on a deserted island, I admit, but to be effective, visualization must be meaningful. I would suggest sitting comfortably, closing your eyes and thinking about the joyful times of your childhood. This is always a good way to bring out the best of you. That child within never dies really; we just stuff him down into a box somewhere and ignore him. Bring him out into the sunshine once in a while; see him playing and "being" there. Find his happy moments. Happiness is the natural human condition. We work hard at being miserable, and the less we succeed the harder we try. Let him show you how easy it really is, and in the process you will learn to visualize. Don't do it with any purpose in mind, just do it. It's a kind of mental masturbation with wonderful rewards. There are many vehicles available to us to learn more about visualizations. The subject is widely used in sales motivation courses and self improvement studies. Check with your local bookstore, or start in the recommended reading list in the back of this book.

TOOL #6
RESISTANCE

Unfortunately, as simple as our goals may sound, the process of attaining them can be very complex, based on our own individual backgrounds. The level of resistance to actually "hearing" on an inner level what we need to hear is a determining factor in the speed and ease with which we move in our chosen direction. Resistance is that place to which we go when our righteousness is challenged. (Righteousness is our protective reaction, when our beliefs are challenged, to avoid being wrong.) If we allow ourselves to accept the possibility that our beliefs may not be written in stone, and that they, like everything else in the universe, is subject to change, our righteousness can be moved aside. Once accomplished, our resistance to hearing will also decrease. Resistance is a blockage in our thinking/feeling process, preventing what we hear from reaching our hearts. Resistance is also the distance, or separation, between what we want and what we have.

Each of us is resistant to different stimuli, to different degrees, of course. The truth is that resistance is no better or no worse than any other human reaction. It just is what it is, and will surface whenever it does. And it may always do so. What determines our success in obtaining our will is our ability to recognize and use resistance as a tool for growth, rather than allowing it to block us. Carrying around a burden of guilt because we are resistant to change does not work either. That is just another form of beating ourselves up. Life is too short, and we are too wonderful to waste so much time in guilt. When resistance surfaces, acknowledge its presence, look at why it is there and move on through, to get to your conscious goals. Visualize yourself already being in the kind of relationships you want. By visualizing what you want you have begun to create it through conscious re-programming.

*Self-knowledge and self-improvement
are very difficult for most people.
It usually needs great courage and
long struggle.*

Abraham Maslow

EXCELLENCE vs. PERFECTION

Excellence is the willingness to be wrong;
Perfection is being right.

Excellence is risk;
Perfection is fear.

Excellence is powerful;
Perfection is anger and frustration.

Excellence is spontaneous;
Perfection is control.

Excellence is accepting;
Perfection is judgment.

Excellence is giving;
Perfection is taking.

Excellence is confidence;
Perfection is doubt.

Excellence is flowing;
Perfection is pressure.

Excellence is journey;
Perfection is destination.

Excellence is surrender;
Perfection is consuming.

Excellence is trust;
Perfection is selfishness.

TOOL #7
EXCELLENCE vs. PERFECTION

A primary factor determining the ease and quickness of our growth is the quality of the energy applied to our goal. Unfortunately, we in America have been heavily dosed with the need for perfection, in order to be perceived as "right." Many of our daily judgments on how we perceive ourselves, as well as others, are based on some arbitrary yardstick of perfection. Our educational system, our employee performance criteria, are, to a large degree, based on someone's idea of perfection, causing needless and excessive amounts of stress in our daily lives. If we look at the options available, a clear line of choice between the elements of perfection vs. excellence becomes evident. I find it very difficult to separate the qualities of righteousness from the conflict inherent in excellence vs. perfection.

On the preceding page is a list of comparisons that you may, or may not have seen before, but which deserves repeating. If they are new to you, I would like to suggest spending some time with them to see how these concepts relate to your life. This list is another of the major tenents of this book. If you have serious doubts about the point of view they represent, look to see if it may be your resistance showing up, and if it is the same attitude that shows up elsewhere in your relationships. These nine concepts are not infallible, but they might represent possibilities not clearly seen from another frame of reference.

The first one, **Excellence is the willingness to be wrong; Perfection is being right,** is the essence of resistance. When we
come into any situation from a position of trying to create perfection, it is saying that we have the only answer for someone else's questions. If we go into the same situation from a commitment to create the best possible results, but willing to accept another person's right to hold a different idea, we come from excellence. The degree to which we protect our need for perfection determines our level of resistance. We rarely have differing levels of resistance in one part of our lives and in another. If we are encountering problems in our close relationships, we are most likely not creating maximum potential in other areas either. It is all a mirror of the amount of resistance we hold to being wrong. Being wrong is an opportunity to learn, and a matter of realizing that it is perfectly fine to be in the moment of opportunity, right or wrong.

At the same time, we rarely approach anything with differing levels of excellence. Excellence comes from a level of commitment that is a way of being, rather than doing, and this is a process that does not turn on and off easily. Resistance is abundant in perfection, manageable in excellence. We can never hope to be completely free of resistance, but we can learn to recognize and control it, rather than have it control us. without a high level of resistance, righteousness cannot exist. Emotional suffering is centered on our resistance to being wrong, or the importance of being right. It goes back to the concept of risk, requiring a willingness to risk being wrong in order to experience growth. As far as relationships go, a simple choice is required: **being right, or having a relationship.**

One thing we all find out very early in the lives of our children is that they react negatively whenever they encounter righteousness. We can be authoritative and effective disciplinarians without being righteous by simply acknowledging a child's right to have an opinion. As long as they realize we know what they feel is important to us, taking suggestion and direction becomes easier.

Authority issues are one of the most common problems encountered in relationships and are almost always father based. Although they can be deeply routed and difficult to treat, often they come from expectations of perfection, which are held by only one of those involved. Perfection is self oriented because it sets up one's own standard as the only "truth". Excellence leaves room for meeting common goals.

Excellence is risk; Perfection is fear. During an earlier discussion of risk, we saw that positive risk is a way of creating movement. In seeking perfection we avoid risk, by setting a single, immovable goal and plowing full force ahead toward attainment, with little regard for those things that do not specifically apply to the goal. This approach insulates us from the unknown, creating a space within which we can operate from absolute control, absolving us of the fear of failure. The irony is that when we set up perfection goals, we are actually setting ourselves up for failure, because perfection, like inner peace, can be only an instant in time/space. At any point we feel we have reached perfection in any task, we find only fleeting satisfaction, leaving us having met a goal but feeling less than complete. The feeling of being incomplete gives us a sense of failure from which compulsion results to set up another level of perfection. There is no argument that this path can achieve great accomplishments in its process, but compulsiveness is living that can only be described as fear of life. This compulsiveness of action and single purposed dedication to goals very often results in massive relationship failure. By taking risks in approaches to goal attainment, we open ourselves to new possibilities, often recognizing solutions unavailable to us under operating conditions of fear. If we allow ourselves to risk a deviation in plan, or an alternative approach, and apply our very best efforts to achieving completion each step along the way, then operating out of excellence is an automatic result. Once excellence in each moment is achieved, our satisfaction becomes a continuous feedback, and peace of mind an ever closer possibility. One could even philosophize on the idea that true perfection is attainable only when excellence in each moment is achieved.

Excellence is powerful; Perfection is anger and frustration. To attack a goal from the perspective of excellence is to be so involved in the *process of doing*, that the goal becomes secondary. When applied to relationships, excellence requires being involved with a person so intensely in the moment that the "need" for the interaction becomes lost in the mechanism. The result is an assumption of immense power within the being. This power comes not with wealth and strength, but is a gentle power that comes from a spiritually based source, an inner knowing of connection with another heart; the kind of power that creates a desire within others to be with you, not jealousy and resentment.

When we enter any exchange with another person from a place of perfection, we are saying that we are interested only in results, and that comes directly from our ego. We have predetermined our intention to make our position the "right" one. Any time we operate from our egos, we set ourselves up for anger and frustration. The ego does not like to be disappointed, setting up expectations of how others will react. If others choose to act otherwise, negative emotions are created within us, and convince us that we have failed. In fact, it is a process of our perception, with little dependence on the inherent quality of the act itself. Allowing the ego to presence itself so dominantly in our actions creates frustrations because we know we are not in control. The power to create exists and lives within all of us, and the recognition and application of this power can lead us down the road to happiness. How far we go is a result of how well we prepare ourselves for the trip.

Excellence is spontaneity; Perfection is control. To be with another in the moment is total spontaneity. Have you ever noticed the difficulty of getting a sense of who a TV newscaster is from his news presentation? We really can't because in most cases he or she is reading the news, not creating. To get a sense of the person on a talk show is far easier because of the spontaneity about the moment of experience. The newscaster's job is based on a level of perfection without room for error. The control factor is dominant. That does not mean he cannot achieve excellence in his presentation; it is a matter of balance, like all things. Control is a wonderful tool, and perhaps the most misused of our gifts. One of the more damaging things we do in our relationships is covertly attempt to control those we love to conform to our expectations of how they should be, rather than respect their right to "just be." Control builds walls. Spontaneity creates space for unlimited possibilities.

Excellence is acceptance; Perfection is judgment. To judge another person is to limit their possibilities. Whenever we make a judgment about someone else or their actions, we do so because we have set up a standard against which we measure their performance. That mental process sets up a continuing series of expectations that are no more valid than the original judgment. Before we realize it, we have determined in our own minds how that person is going to act, under a given set of circumstances. Unfortunately, expectation is a creative process, and often we live up to these expectations, or what we believe others expect of us, even when we are capable of more. The secret, if there is one, to having relationships work, is in accepting everyone exactly as they are, and allowing them a supportive space in which they can reach their potential. This is not a possible result in the atmosphere of judgment. The trick is in learning to accept the fact that judgement exists in each of us, and needs only to be acknowledged, and set aside so that we may interact with others on a productive basis.

Excellence is giving; Perfection is taking. There are two ways of being with others, giving or taking. We are all givers and takers to differing degrees at different times, but each of us is mostly one or the other most of the time. Most of us are takers, in the sense that we get wrapped up in our own problems, forgetting that those around us exist too, and by definition, not giving is taking. Not taking is not necessarily giving, but not taking can be taking. We see this demonstrated in love. When we do not give our love to another, we lose it because love can only be given. If we do not give it away, we take it from ourselves, and it dissipates into the universe, unused. If we spend our lives waiting for the right person, or a person to live up to our standards, if that person does ever show up, we've lost the ability to create a giving and loving relationship. When we operate from excellence, we learn to love whatever we have for exactly what it is, as it is. Love in no way limits our possibilities, but creates a joyous and constantly expanding life.

Excellence is confidence; Perfection is doubt. To approach any endeavor from a need for perfection, one must be filled with doubt about the ability to create alternative possibilities. If one can work toward a goal, doing the best he can in each moment, the constant reinforcement of each moment's success will build a lasting level of confidence that becomes a way of life.

Excellence is flow. Perfection is pressure. As we move from one moment into another with a sense of committed presence, we literally flow through life, experiencing multi-faceted aspects of our emotional being. Within the moment, we can feel the pain, anxiety, frustration, joy, anticipation, excitement, all the qualities that make up our senses, knowing that in the next instant something completely different can appear. Nothing really changes except our perspective, but the results on our quality of life can be amazing. When we aim for perfection anything that comes into our path that may deter us from a single-minded goal, creates pressure because we do not want to be side-tracked. The result is devastating on relationships, because no one likes to be put aside in favor of a goal.

Excellence is journey; Perfection is destination.
What can I say?

Excellence is surrender; Perfection is consumption.
In search of perfection, all the energy available to us, is consumed, not only our own, but from anyone who is in the way. We cannot help ourselves. We see life's goals as worth justifying the means, whatever they may be. In excellence, we become part of the flow of life, taking in whatever each moment brings to us, and acting on it to expand our limits. Surrender is allowing our senses to create our responses; following what we feel should be done for the greatest good, not necessarily what we planned to do for the greatest gain. Surrender allows us to know that whatever happens, it will turn out to be exactly what is needed.

Excellence is trust. Perfection is selfishness.
On the road to perfection we can only be concerned with our ultimate desire. All other interests become secondary to the task at hand. We use whatever we need to get to where we want to go, thereby becoming consumptive takers.

Trust is that quality that allows us to give space to others, that they may reach their own level of excellence. Selfishness is protecting that which we have or plan to attain, because we believe these things are who we are, and without them we are nothing.

Trusting our intuition is what getting in touch with our inner self is about. By operating from the inner knowledge that there is only the now, one can look at self-imposed expectations in a different light. Perfection is an anomaly; one of those philosophical arguments that can be one thing, and its opposite, at the same time. If there is only the now, then perfection at any level can never be attained, because perfection is thought to come as a result of repetition, doing something until it is "perfect." Perfection can also be said to exist only for an instant, because it is a component of an ever-changing universe; therefore those criteria by which perfection might be judged are always changing. Then there is the belief that we are all absolutely perfect, at any given moment in time, because we are sacred. Anyway one looks at it, perfection is a difficult way to achieve happiness in one's life.

These concepts concerning perfection and excellence are, as we normally use language, contradictory, but equally valid and able to exist in our lives beautifully concurrently. If we visualize ourselves as always perfect, on a journey of growth and expansion, toward greater perfection in each moment on a higher level of wisdom and knowledge, our lives can become far more manageable. We can then know that failure will occur in our lives. Mistakes will be made. Errors in judgment will abound. But if we see ourselves as always growing, always learning, we can accept those events that many of us experience as problems, and see them as opportunities to expand positively. Then and only then can we look at our sons in the same light. When we can accept our own vulnerabilities as being part of the human condition and not a result of it, we can help them develop positive self-images. This is not to say that we can look at our misdeeds, forgive them as being perfect at the time, and go out and do them again. Each moment and each event that comes to us is part of our opportunity to learn. Our choice is whether we choose to learn or not. The rocky road of perfection, or the rocky road of excellence? The difference is we do one in a Jeep, and the other in a BMW.

What we resist, persists.
Resistance is the root cause of all pain.
Resistance of any kind is violence.
Suffering is caused by our resistance,
and based on our judgments, beliefs and
being right.
There is always resistance when direction
comes from outside of self.

Human potentials training jargon

ENERGY FORMS

MASCULINE	FEMININE
Aggressive	Flowing
Powerful	Subtle
Rigid	Soft
Closed	Open
Dominant	Supportive
Negative	Positive
Serious	Playful
Grounded	Lightness
Anxiety	Surrender
Pressure	Forgiving
Perfection	Excellence
Righteousness	Harmlessness
Control	Spontaneity
Judgment	Acceptance
Taking	Giving
Doubt	Confidence
Consuming	Allowing
Anger	Joy
Left brain	Right brain
Selfishness	Trust
Winter	Spring
Fall	Summer
Yang	Yin
Analy	Synthetical
Verbal	Visual

These are grouped by their absolute forms of definition, and may cross over, depending on the situation. However, they are listed here to point out their intrinsic energy values.

TOOL# 8
THE MASCULINE/FEMININE CONNECTION

If you think there's any doubt about this being a feminine planet, forget it! We call her Mother Earth just for starters, and many power images we create are referred to in the feminine gender. We even refer to our cars as feminine, as in "start her up!" Our tools of war, work and pleasure, and until the women's rights movement, even hurricanes were named in the feminine. It's no wonder that on a subconscious, if not conscious, level, we men wander around looking for some form of self connectedness. One of the women's movement's great gripes, chauvinism, is often a compensating overreaction, in which the male uses aggressive behavior to attain love and attention not obtainable in any other way. Aggression results when on an inner level a man feels that women hold a greater power than he or somehow threatens his. Power is not a question of holding, but of balancing, as measured in terms of feminine / masculine energy. In many instances it is a combination of environmental and traditional exposures that were first expressed in classic behavioral patterns. The mother first, and then the wife have been the dominant figures in most men's lives. Many of these women want desperately to adjust this energy imbalance, as it serves the women no better than the men.

One way of doing this, of course, is to reverse the roles of husband and wife within the family structure, and for a few this has proven to be a successful path. However, even this "solution" maintains a relationship in an out-of-balance condition, just in the opposite direction. The mother role needs to be supported by the father/son combination, not in a service position, but as one of importance within the family structure, equal to everyone. During the seventies many women ran fruitless campaigns to create federal acknowledgment of mothering services by trying to place monetary values on their services. The rigidity and formality of our basically masculine power structure would not allow this to occur, and this immobility is typical of the masculine energy form. More masculine energy, in the form of aggressive women, only solidified the resistance to risking the change.

One way to achieve an understanding of how this energy system works is to risk the loss of some of these traditional concepts of how things are **supposed** to be, and orient oneself to finding things that work. Perhaps a planned program of shared household responsibilities based not on historical roles, but on what works, depending on availability and preferences. Reversing responsibility just for the sake of making a role change accomplishes little, because a masculine energy environment called conflict usually results. If the anxiety (which is the natural result of too much masculine energy) is reduced, and feminine energy in the form of willingness to move off of rigid beliefs can be substituted, a working environment can be readily established, which represents a better balance of energies. Keep in mind we are talking about basic relationships, and as we have seen, these relationships hold their own separate identities and energy, greater than that of their components. By creating a condition wherein everyone committed to the relationship is interacting in a positive manner, opportunities for success are increased many times. In fact, the potential of creating space for success where none may have existed at all is excellent. It is all a matter of recognizing when the energy patterns shift from the negative, hard-ine masculine form, to the open softness of the feminine form, and accepting them as opportunities rather than challenges.

This new understanding of feminine energy is making us aware of options for making change. It is fine to want to change the way we live, and to want to make our lives and all of our relationships work better, but we must also have the tools with which to do the work. I have seen and felt this tremendous increase in feminine energy, but this is not a prerequisite for putting the concept to work in one's life. If your relationship with your son, daughter, husband, wife, parent, friend or anyone is not what you want it to be, look at the quality of the energy being created in it, and apply some new direction in the form of new energy. Take a risk! It's the only life you have. The female in each of us, man or woman, deeply wants to love and care. That bit of female energy in each of us needs to be nurtured, developed and used, or, like an unused muscle, it will wither and die. A willingness to risk, for many reading this, is necessary to put these ideas into action. Go to your feelings and know that your sons and their mothers are you, and that in your inner wisdom, you know what needs to be done. Bonding with your son is the process of the mother within you connecting with mutual need. Once you have learned how to have one successful relationship, you can have a successful relationship with anyone you choose. The secret is simple. Just accept the belief that each of us has lessons to learn and they can be learned while allowing others to learn theirs. A mother knows this instinctively. We so often want to "help" those we love by pushing our life experiences on them. Letting go of this need to project is difficult, but it is needed in order truly to allow growth around us.

The mother in us wants everything to be "perfect," and we try to control everyone around us in our masculine way to make it be that way. The mother in us knows that everything is already as perfect as it needs to be, in the moment, to support the lessons needed to be learned.

*When it is dark enough,
you can see the stars.*

Ralph Waldo Emerson

TOOL# 9
PROBLEMS vs. OPPORTUNITIES

"There are no problems, only opportunities." I have no idea who first coined this phrase, but no concept in my own life has meant more to my mental, physical, spiritual and emotional growth. In years of running a fairly good sized manufacturing business, operating from this idea allowed me to stay with a problem long enough to solve it by knowing that in every instance an opportunity to learn something new was presented. By instilling the concept in the work force, an environment was created where quality and pride of workmanship were the natural result of people recognizing their responsibility to see opportunities in problem solving.

I suspect that some of you reading this would like to give me a couple of your "opportunities" right now, and see how I do! True, it is often difficult to see the opportunity, but never the less, it always exists. Like many other ideas or beliefs held, it is not that problems actually hold a specific energy solution, but that they create movement. What I do know is that belief works, and if you believe a problem is insolvable, it is! Too often we accept a given belief, and do not consider alternative possibilities. It takes risk to go beyond our limiting beliefs and create new truth. If you take what has been presented so far, and apply just these ideas to your insolvable problems, you will find many new possibilities opening up. Unconditional love; allowing others to learn their own lessons; risking and openness to possibilities without fear, will each impart its own effect on your problems.

Let us look, for example, at a problem of a youngster who lies and steals excessively. Both of these activities are fundamental to deep trouble developing. Often lying and stealing represent a lack of self worth, poor self image and severe responsibility issues. The quality of our success in parenting is a combination of experience, instinct, and accepting responsibility. When a child begins manifesting dysfunctional symptoms, he's reacting to outside stimuli. Perhaps he's looking for attention from absent parents or broken marriages. The reason may be important, but you cannot correct past mistakes. What is done is done, and all the guilt trips we exercise, all the psychiatric help, counseling and self analysis in the world won't change what is.

The stimulation to move us into clearer waters is "what do we do about it?" The opportunity existing here is of immense importance. When our children exhibit anti-social signals, or any other of like significance, they are yelling as loud as they can, "Excuse me, but I need some attention," and they are giving us the opportunity to give it. We must be willing to risk some of our old belief patterns. Not give them up to someone else's ideas but risk enough to find out if we can do better. Go to your son and his problems, and experience unconditional love with him. Tell him that no matter what happens you love him, and nothing he does is going to change that. **Ever!** Tell him his problems are as much yours as his because he is only an extension of you, and you would like to help him and yourself at the same time. Even our kids like to know that they have something of value to teach. This does not mean that you give up your responsibility as a disciplinarian. You can punish a child, and still allow him to see the need for him to take himself and his own responsibilities seriously.

It's not just one kid out there screaming. It's all of them. It's women seeking equality; it's fouled water; polluted air; the nuclear arsenal! The world! And if we don't listen now, our old belief patterns are going to blow our beloved planet apart. These are clear options. Think about it.

IF IT IS TO BE, IT'S UP TO ME.

Much of this book was written while traveling around the western United States. From my home in Sedona Arizona, I visited many of the "power spots" in New Mexico Arizona, Mexico and California. These are areas in which the natural beauty of the land accesses the right brain with extreme ease. As we observed earlier, the connection of the male to the wilderness goes deeply into the roots of his identity. I am convinced that the connection is to the primal memory at the cellular level. Women, of course, are sensitive to this draw, but generally less so and the appeal is to their masculine energy side. The following details my own feelings at one of these points of wonder.

The Grand Canyon:
Sitting here on the edge of the Colorado River, on a 1.5 billion-year-old piece of pink granite, it's easy to get lost in the time-space vacuum. Insignificance here is easy. We talk about today's problems and opportunities and now they seem so absolutely non existent, against the framework of this "grand" canyon. If one is ever truly to understand the significance of the "now,"

this place will do it. But here, in the inner-most depths of the canyon, where the first rays of the sun don't hit till midmorning, it strikes me that it's the same water, the same eternity, the same wonder that exists here, that exists when the spring rain flows gently down the curbs in New York City, Washington, D.C., or Crawfordsville, Indiana. The only difference is what the water is doing in its moment. One, great and majestic in its mass and power. One, unnoticed and passive, but still, on the same journey, the circle of life. So it is with us, in our fleeting moment on earth. This moment is all we have. Use it to its fullest potential. Don't let your relationships drift to a place you don't want them to be without doing your part.

Mother Nature has many lessons for us, but as long as we lock ourselves up in our cities and factories we won't learn them. Go out into the sun, into the mountains, the deserts, the canyons, with your son or father or brother. Experience what it is to fear the night unprotected by the glass and plaster womb that would be your mother but never can be. Feel the wind and the rain as they wash away the poisons of civilization and free the inner self to explore the wonder that is God, that is the God within us all. Here is where the real man resides and waits only to be found, where true inner peace can be touched, and bathed in. This is where we learn to solve problems, break the hold of drugs and alcohol and get to see ourselves as whole and wondrous and beautiful. We are men with much to learn, and we have friends and fathers and sons to learn our lessons with, so that our women may profit.

*If fate throws a knife at you,
there are two ways of catching it
-by the blade, or by the handle-*

fortune cookie

TOOL #10
DEFINING THE MALE

I have discovered that there are as many definitions of maleness as there are people to ask. However, some common ideals seem to have survived the tests of time. Physical strength and endurance appear at the top of most lists. These attributes manifest themselves in many other areas, covering virility, responsibility, etc. As we come closer to what is called the point of maximum absorption on the planet, the need for greater masculine/feminine balance becomes critically important.

As in all cyclical development, experiencing the extremes of these energies is necessary before a balance can be recognized. We can only know what something is if we have experienced what it is not. Thus far, on this planet, we not only have experienced the extremes of gender separation, we've been stuck in it for centuries. Personally, I do not believe the purely androgenous or asexual position of religious, spiritual or secular groups to be any more in balance than pure feminism or violent chauvinism. Sexuality is a major common tenent of the universal oneness. Sexuality is the one expression of love most easily recognizable, and therefore the one place we most easily go to find love. That doesn't mean love is there to find, it just means we think so. Aside from the procreation aspect, sexuality is an ego function. Because we are embodied in a physical form that supports sexuality through a highly developed sensory system, to deny our sexuality on any level is to deny a part of our existence that is absolute in the process of continuing our kind. Sexuality, then, is not a function of masculinity in any greater degree than in femininity, but a core of life itself. So on that basis, we can remove sexuality from our definition of masculinity. Without reference to sexual functions, I suspect many of us would have a lot more difficulty in our definition of masculinity.

The term "maximum absorption" was used a little earlier, and to define this concept here is important, in order to understand fully the idea of maleness as it relates to the "now" experience. The population of this planet, and its ability to change its chemical balance through recombining elements and the resultant waste factor, has brought humanity to the point at which our atmosphere can no longer purify itself through natural means. At some point, and many will argue we are already there, we must take responsibility for balancing the harmony of our natural state. Water is one of the prime examples. This planet has the capacity to create a maximum amount of water.

Once we've poisoned that supply with our chemicals and waste, we just can't get any more. There is no place to go for it. We can add more and more filtration and chemicals, but some of the chemicals won't filter and many are not biodegradable, which means they remain in our bodies. However, eventually these chemicals must go somewhere, and only two choices are available. They can be buried or put into the air, where in either case there is no way to guarantee they won't show up again in our food or drink. In fact, we can pretty well guarantee that they **will** show up sooner or later. The point at which the planet can no longer "hide" these toxins I call the "point of maximum absorption." I subscribe to the belief that we've been there for quite some time.

So, you may be asking with impatience, what does this have to do with maleness? Well quite a bit, actually. Of the definitions I've looked at, the one that becomes more and more obvious is very simply, "being responsible." Taking responsibility for our own actions is a basic element of the masculine side of both sexes. Responsibility is action in its purest form. The more in touch we are with our masculine side, the more maleness manifests itself in active energy and "groundedness." From this we can begin to look at definitions in terms of energy rather than words. The application of "masculine responsibility energy" to our relationship with our sons will transfer through the nuclear family to our society. When enough people within that society carry a high enough level of responsibility, the transference once again becomes synergistic. Before long, we and our sons will have been responsible for having saved the earth. And, in the meantime, the journey will have filled our lives with love, excitement and fun. Absorption in our own masculinity and femininity will help bring all energies into better balance. This is why the father/son relationship is one key to the future of the planet. In truth it doesn't matter if it's father/son, father/daughter, or any other combination of relationships. What matters is the energy balance existing between beings and that it is recognized for what it can create, with minimum negative interference from the active ego.

This experience is what the land brings to us. The Native American culture has expressed it for countless generations, and we have much to learn from their beliefs. Take our sons out onto the land and be **one** with Mother Earth **together**, on the mountain, at the shore, in the wilderness. Without the earth, we cannot live. We and the land are both sacred. This is where we discover what maleness and femaleness are. This is where responsibility to mankind swells up and becomes real, where one gets the knowledge of what is really important in life. *In this context, maleness can be said to be a state of understanding; an appreciation of those qualities that allow us to function successfully in harmony with nature, not in conflict with it.*

*There are no facts,
only interpretations.*

Nietzsche

TOOL #11
LOOKING WITHIN

Part of the traditional European-American concept of gender definition revolves around the traditions themselves. As cultures became more efficient, environmental as well as social assimilation changed mankind's responses, and the traditions have had to fight hard to survive. Some have succeeded, some have not, but many have had significant influence over the "now" of our lives. Among these are inherited social status, religions and cultural bias based on hard-formed belief systems. Of primary importance is one that can cross many lines of definition, that being the tendency to look outside of ourselves for solutions to problems for which we refuse to take responsibility. When our kids "go bad," we blame the generation gap, easy availability of drugs, the moral deterioration of our society and anything else we can find that fits into our rationalization pattern. It may be quite impossible for any "society" to do anything, including deteriorate. A "society" is really nothing - only a word to which we have given an immensely important arbitrary meaning. It is the people within the society who are the society. So when we blame society for anything, we are blaming ourselves. Most of us don't like to look at it that way, of course, because then guess who gets to share the responsibility? Suddenly "we" are part of "them." Because we have convinced ourselves that "we" are separate from "them," we can be helpless and therefore guilt free.

That is called looking without, and is the reason why so many contemporary relationships don't work. Looking without is the foundation of expectation. If you truly desire to beat yourself to death mentally, physically and emotionally, really get into expectation. When we expect a certain level of performance from another human being, we set ourselves up for disappointment. What if that person's level of excellence is different from ours? He or she then becomes wrong just because they disagree with us. What's worse is that we run a very high risk of becoming invested in being "right." If you are in a situation where the performance level of another person is vital to the relationship, the responsibility is yours to make that known to him/her. It then becomes a matter of choice whether he/she wants to follow the same path with you, move to a new path, or perhaps create a different path together. The relationship is not found in where you are going, but in how you handle the journey. When you and your son disagree about the path to be followed, give him the unconditional love he needs to make his choices. Do this by knowing that your answers may not be his answers, but he can't find out without trusting his own inner knowing. Your ability to allow him to trust his knowing is directly related to how you trust yours.

So you see, nothing exists in a vacuum. We can't give our sons information and support if we don't have a similar foundation in our own life. Your son looks at how you live your life, and because his options are so plentiful, the chances are that he will not follow in your footsteps, as he might have done in times past. But he will know how you have been operating. What he needs from you is not his food, but seed to plant on his own land. If food is what he wants, he'll plant the seed. Your inner knowing is a testament to how you operate in the now. If you trust your ability to survive this moment in excellence, you will, and if you trust that this moment is all there is, your life will improve at a phenomenal rate, one moment at a time. If you're stuck in your moment worrying about yesterday's mistakes, consumed by guilt, or worrying about the problems that **may** come up tomorrow, you're lost. Life will pass away with you having been an event in other people's moment, but having missed your own. One of my favorite quotes is, (and I wish I knew to whom to attribute it)," **Life** is what happens while you're planning for the future." Life does not happen "out there", it happens within.

Very often in our sexual relationships, we run into the same kind of problem. We look to our partners for fulfillment. If we think about it, we can see that they just couldn't possibly give fulfillment to us. They don't have it to give! How can a woman possibly satisfy a man's sexual needs, or visa versa. Each provides his or her own fulfillment based on the degree and quality of the energy within the relationship, **in that moment!** Even when a relationship is based purely on sex, the level of satisfaction, which is only passing anyway, will be directly related to how fully the partners are committed to each other **in that moment.**

The same can be said for our relationships with our kids. Children cannot be looked to as a source of satisfaction for the parents. They can only be the stimulus and the recipient of it. The satisfaction comes from within our own systems, and is a function of our own expectations based on our belief systems.

All too often our expectations of our kids, when not met, result in anger. Expectation and anger are common bedfellows. Adults seldom realize that children live in a totally different paradigm than they do. We can relate to the child's paradigm because at least for most of us, we have been there and advanced through it. They, however, cannot relate to ours. A simple illustration is telling a three-year-old he must wait two hours until dinner time. Two hours is a reasonable time period for mom, who must clean the kitchen, do some errands and then cook the meal.

To the three-year-old who is just beginning to develop a comprehension of time, two hours is a significant percentage of his/her life. Although only a simple example, interactions like these often cause unavoidable frustration; but some simple awareness can make it easier. First, psychiatrists tell us that only about the 5 percemt of the feelings of anger that we feel toward anyone in a given situation has anything at all to do with that situation. The anger comes from our own deeply suppressed and non-released anxieties, generally from childhood. Our own angers surface when we are emotionally cornered and we express it on our children. They, of course, have no way of understanding that, and become convinced that they are the cause of our anger, making them wrong, bad, etc. Men react in a similar way to children when confronted with situations they do not know how to handle emotionally. We shut down emotionally and literally are unable to communicate. When we are called upon to express our emotions we generally make a shambles of it because our programming has not made it socially acceptable to experience them. Our ideas of masculinity leave no room for expression. When children are yelled at they generally sulk, sob and put their bodies into protective and inward focused positions. Watch them the next time you find yourself either expressing anger or are present when someone else is yelling at their kids. Men do the same, only on an interior level, not allowing it to show. We must tough it out. The anger is stuffed again, a little deeper until eventually it explodes, as it must. The human system is not capable of holding a full lifetime of suppressed emotions.

Women follow similar patterns, but because crying and released anger are acceptable feminine behavior, it generally creates a supportive response. They express emotion more readily and more often. This single feminine attribute is, I believe, the single most important difference in the way men and women live, and its effect on the family is total.

The family dynamic and its degree of dysfunction is a subject that could and does fill volumes. There is no way to attempt a complete coverage of all the important factors that affect men today. Considering the premise that it takes the same qualities to create successful relationships, regardless of who is involved in them, it is helpful to look at the significance of whole family interaction. It is difficult, as we have looked at before, to segregate emotional responses within the family core. Anger, frustration, insensitivity and inadequate communication will always lead to marital problems that affect the children.

SEX

One of the first signs of marital problems is the advent of sexual problems. Such problems are only rarely of a physical nature, but usually the result of stress in other areas of the relationship that get transferred to the sexual arena. Men need to go to their inner awareness here, because sex is the area where men are most vulnerable, and women the most reactive. Because so many of us equate our sexuality with our maleness, any damage to our operating belief systems in this area creates a need for compensating sexual activity. We feel the need to prove our maleness through sex because we do not realize that maleness has nothing to do with sex. What happens is that a masculine energy flow is created: that of aggressiveness, aborting the feminine energy flow of love, tenderness, and compassion. If a man truly wants sexual fulfillment as a part of "his now," it's a matter of learning to go inside and tap his feminine side, in order to approach his mate with an energy flow **she** can understand. Once the problems in a relationship get so intense that this is no longer a viable process, the resistance level will require outside counseling if a solution is to be achieved. There is no difference with our kids. Once a condition of aggressive resistance is reached, we cannot afford to wait for **"them"** to grow **out** of it. The lesson is that these are the times for **us** to grow **into** the possibility for solution. When we move into the energy flow of the sons and daughters in a way that they can relate to, then communication can begin. Understanding our energy flows can help achieve that awareness. Outside advice and information may be helpful, but the answers are not out there; they are inside, and the responsibility to find them belongs to us.

Women need also to realize that most men enjoy being approached on their maleness level, and it can be wonderfully beneficial to a relationship for the women to be sensitive to the energy flows of their mates by being aggressive sexually when that is appropriate. Men also want to be wanted. If we make love to our partner, as though the love making were part of the relationship, rather than something we do to each other, this sexual interaction will work better. Again, it goes back to visualizing the relationship as a viable entity all its own, needing to be nourished and supported independently. Less a question of whose sexual satisfaction is at stake, and more a matter of the success of the relationship. Today's society has made it very easy for us to go outside both ourselves and our relationships for answers. Our religious institutions have always been great examples, particularly in the more orthodox factions.

I certainly am not anti-religion, but historically, the dogma of classic Judaic-Christian thought has been aimed at control of the human condition through fear, discipline and obedience, rather than freedom of will. A national trend does seem to be developing today that acknowledges and allows far easier access to alternate belief systems, which in return, may create less need for support through traditional dogma. We have recognized that there can be many different answers to a given question, without a requirement for any of the answers to be wrong in order for one to be right. More and more people seem to be willing to accept the possibilities presented by alternative solutions.

The abundance of self-help and mutual support groups such as A.A., Alanon, Parents Without Partners, Big Brothers/Big Sisters, Lifespring, Forum, Outward Bound, Inward Bound, single issue weekend seminars by the thousands, singles groups, professional trade organizations of all kinds, and an enormous increase in esoteric and metaphysical interest, bear witness to the reluctance of many people to accept single source, dogmatic answers. The more options we have, the more information we apply to our decisions. Then, once we have adequate information, we can address the process of determining how we feel vs. how we **think** we feel about an issue. I personally can see the day coming when American corporations will make responsibility for such learning environments a top priority, and make them available for their employees.

*Most people look at the measure
of love from what they are
getting out of it. True love
comes from what you put into it.*

anonymous

TOOL #12
FEELING vs. THINKING

Science has known for a long time that the human brain functions as a two-part unit. The left and right halves, known oddly enough as the left brain and right brain, are thought to have very different functions. The left brain controls our conscious thought, logic, and motor functions. The right, our intuition, emotions and feelings. Hence, one who operates from an intellectual, analytical place is said to be left-brained, and one who is highly emotional or intuitively directed is right-brained. Of course, each side has many functions other than these; both play a critical role in survival, and clearly, although each of us tends to be directed predominantly from one side or the other, our lives generally seem to want us to create a balance between the two.

Many of the human potential trainings available today use this drive for balance as a foundation for growth. In America, as in other industrial societies, we have a dominant left-brain orientation. We can analyze, project, calculate and postulate better and longer than any culture in history. Where we have found real problems is in feeling. The left brain understands sharing of deep, moving experiences and values created when others become aware that we can experience how they feel under certain conditions, because we have felt those very same feelings. We can never really "feel" what other people are feeling, but we can and do "experience" their reactions.

Right-brain awareness has the capability to expose us to many possibilities unheard of or unacceptable to our normally conscious understanding. As we surround ourselves with the process and products of this mechanistic information age, our left brain hypnotizes us into believing that we are our results in life. Our cultural system rewards us for results, rather than the process that produces the results. Our educational system, our parental attitudes, virtually every aspect of contemporary society rewards results. This is a fine and natural process, and has created immense advances in nearly every country in the world, and in every area of human activity. The problem is that this process may have worked too well. We tend to look at our results as being definitions of who we are. When our youngsters, in their desire to please, take on a task for us which may be beyond their limits of physical or intellectual expertise, they view themselves as a success/failure based on our expectations of them. They become their results in both their image and ours. We often make mental judgments about who our children are very early in their lives, and reinforce our views of them on them. Then when they reach an age where their true talents and abilities begin to show in a different direction, we label them rebellious and unappreciative. That child who we were convinced had genius level gifts in dance at age four, and spent thousands of dollars on dancing lessons, blows our lives apart when at age eighteen she or he announces a desire to study anthropology. Our left brain has conditioned us to perceive one another in ways that may well be inconsistent with the development of the right brain.

In truth, our results are only one measure of who we are. Who we really are is a mix of many beliefs and attitudes **about** ourselves, built up over our lifetime. **You, we, the I am, the self,** that is at the core of each of us, our own individual essence, is the same for every human on the face of the earth who is, ever has been or ever will be. By viewing life and relationships, knowing that every child who dies of starvation, bullet wound or neglect, is the same as you and I and therefore part of us, the right brain will automatically be drawn into consciousness. Berating or withholding love or support from another, is also doing the same to yourself, and feeding the ego, which lives in the left brain.

Many of the ancient religions, as well as those of the Native Americans, believe that the expression of oneness is contained in all things, living or dead. The Native American sees the Great Spirit as the creator or overseer of Father Sky and Mother Earth. All other things are held within those two areas, and all are connected through the heart. All things are the same, having merely taken differing forms of visible energy patterns. To harm anyone or anything is to harm oneself at some level. If everything created by God is sacred, each of us is sacred and all things are sacred. Whether or not we can bring our left brain to accept these ideas is a function of how much we are interested in challenging our current existence. The validity, from a religious or cultural point of view, is our choice to make, but what a wonderful way to run our lives. We cannot and should not stop the development of the left brain, or the controlled expansion of man's mechanized world, but we must learn to find more ways to integrate the right brain's intuitive, humanitarian side, as part of the whole brain experience.

Mother Earth and Mother Nature have provided us with an abundance of resources and opportunities to develop our civilizations. These feminine energies are now in high resistance, forcing us to look at our failure to integrate our feelings and inner knowing to keep the planet in balance. The resistance is being manifested through such ecological disasters as the deterioration of the ozone layer, worldwide weather pattern changes, recurring El Ninos, and droughts. Some would even point to increased levels of volcanic and earthquake activities, as signs of nature's dissatisfaction. As we discussed earlier, the planet cannot absorb any further waste and chemical disrespect and still continue providing us with the abundance we have come to expect.

To relate this to our sons, consider the possibility that the sons are learning, as did their fathers, from their own experience. It is essential that they have support, through unconditional love, to resist being their results, and concentrate on their processes, from a right-brain perspective. Your son could be the one who fulfills mankind's dream of peace, or the one who pushes the final button. That's our legacy, our choice, our responsibility. Just thinking about problems won't **do** anything. Feeling the importance of the responsibility to mankind is the creative energy that will make it happen. Without movement there can be no growth; without growth, no future; with no future, no need for this moment of now. Thought is energy without motion. The movement process is that which converts the benign energy to active. One is of no value without the other. Both are needed to make movement happen. The ancient Oriental philosophers called it Yin and Yang, the contemporary term is balance. Whatever you see it as, our Mother Earth is being forced to operate in unequal proportions of giving and taking, and she is in pain.

There isn't enough darkness in all the world to snuff out the light of one little candle.

Anonymous

TOOL #13
MEDITATION

There are many ways to get in touch with our feelings. For most of us, it is not an easy or comfortable process. Commitment is necessary to be part of the future and responsible for the now. Required is a willingness to risk well developed levels of comfort created for self protection. A good way to start getting in touch is through the meditation process. Stop for a moment and take a look at what went through your system when you read that word "meditation." Many have some very rigid beliefs about this practice, connecting it with cults, shaved heads, monasteries and California "weirdoes." (Although they're not only in California anymore). I'm not going to suggest that you shave your head, or tithe 50 percent of your salary to some organization with a thirty-year program of divine connectedness, although if you choose to do that, that is your choice. What I am going to suggest is that you take a look at meditation in a new way. Meditation in its simplest form is merely concentrating the awake and aware mind on one single thought or object. That's all. This concentration releases the tension and stress of the left brain control and allow the right brain an opportunity to kick in and express itself. You've probably been meditating most of your life, and never knew it because your belief about meditation was not consistent with your experience of it. Who has never "spaced out," or been driving along on their daily commute and suddenly became aware that for the several moments, they were doing and thinking absolutely nothing on a conscious level? That's automatic meditation. Our brain is smarter than we give it credit for, thank God. It knows the value of using both of its sides and it does it sometimes, whether we want it to or not. It appears that most if not all of our creative thought comes through this right brain processing. The more relaxed the right brain is, the easier it is for it to function, and meditation can be a very effective form of relaxation. When you're working through a tough analytical problem, your left brain uses all its input and energy to develop a solution. If there is a missing link in the equation, the left brain cannot "create" or fill that link. Its job is processing billions of bits of data collected through our senses, but it does not "create" to fill the unknown. You work and struggle, pump down the coffee, rumple your hair, bite your nails, and still the solution escapes you, so you take a break and do something of a completely different nature and energy flow. Then the right brain kicks in and sends the left a shot of creative juice, and bingo, you get the solution. (This is a highly simplified version of what actually happens, for the

113

purpose of maintaining the flow of the theme, and is easily the subject of its own book.) What has been described is a meditative process, although admittedly a stretched one from the purist's point of view. The process shows us, however, that when we give the right brain a chance to contribute, it will. Through meditation, we can actually learn to control the flow of right brain contribution.

There is still a great deal we do not know about how the brain functions, and it has been suggested that the two halves are genetically programmed not to work together, so that the separateness of function can be maintained. Experiments and studies in recent years with what are called "split-brain" patients, however, have tended to support the view that each half works in a complementary fashion, each with its own specialized area of input, but able to function completely and separately. In her wonderfully informative book, **Drawing on the Right Side of the Brain**, Betty Edwards details some of these studies in which hopelessly uncontrollable epileptics had the area between the two halves that acts as the connector, called the corpus callosum, totally severed surgically, and were restored to a nearly perfect functioning level. This with both halves operating completely separately.

Through meditation, we can learn to control the flow of right brain contribution. I have tried many different forms of meditation, and one that seems to work best for me is the simplest. I spend from five to 45 minutes, depending on where I am in the moment. Just sit in a comfortable and quiet place, on a chair that will support the back in a straight-up position, so that the spine supports the weight of the head.

Close the eyes and simply concentrate on breathing, just in and out, in and out. You can say the words "in and out," or count, "one two, one two." It really doesn't matter, as long as you do the same thing. There is no right or wrong way to meditate, but simply a matter of finding the inner process that works best for you. Easy breathing will quiet the inner noises, and as the thoughts keep coming into your mind, and they will, just acknowledge their presence and go back to being aware of your breath. Within a very short period of time, you'll recognize a new level of inner peace and natural quietness that opens up the left brain and allows the right to flow in with new options, solutions and possibilities.

Another wonderful form of meditation is being with what the Native American calls mother earth. Just walking the land. You have probably many times felt the all-consuming pleasure and relaxed state of mind resulting from a walk in a park or wooded area, or even from driving through such a delightful scene. The process is very simple, the pleasures and rewards vital. The only requirement is that you love yourself enough to give yourself the time.

The major problem in getting a meditative program started is the discipline required to make it effective. Recognizing meditation is as natural to us as breathing, it will require only the desire to make it a formal part of everyday life. Just spending fifteen minutes, twice a day for two weeks, doing a disciplined meditation program will allow a tremendous change in reaction experience to outside stimuli, on an emotional basis. What's even better is that you will notice that those around you will react in an analogous manner. Your calmness will have a soothing effect on others. Meditation is another tool that, when seriously used, can affect not only your relationships at the time, but in the totality of your life. Stress reduction effects of meditation have been used for centuries, and are known and practiced by the world's largest corporations and many successful people. The less stress, the more effective are the intrapersonal relationships, and a far happier life is the possibility. Children generally regard meditation as being a little strange. Sooner or later, your children's experiences of you, after you've meditated on a mutual conflict, will probably show some movement in his or her belief systems, about the practice. The results of dealing with the conflict from a relaxed, creative position will speak for themselves. Our thought manifests itself in our reality. The warm tear of relaxed acceptance is a signal that the two spheres of our brain are working together, and the masculine-feminine energies are coming into balance.

I find that music can be a fantastic aid to meditation. Most music stores carry what is called "new age" music, much of which is slow, relaxed instrumental, designed to relax the mind and body. There are also available many prerecorded guided meditations that serve the same purpose. Experiment and find the best way for you, but don't ignore the possibility that meditation has for you.

Loneliness is the way by which destiny endevors to lead man to himself.

Herman Hesse

A VISION QUEST:

a communion with spirit
a guiding
a journey, an adventure, a pilgrimage
a shedding of the old
a dying/rebirth
a meeting with yourself alone
a rite of passage
a seeking beyond ordinary sight
a crying for a vision
a severance from daily life
a transition with spirit
a return realizing internal changes

TOOL #14
RITES OF PASSAGE

Throughout history in almost every known civilization, the male has participated in a "rite of passage." Originally a pagan celebration of manhood and fertility, it has contemporary counterparts in most modern religions and cultures, except current Western society. Traditionally it was through this process that the formal passing on of manhood and with it the responsibilities of power and leadership were given to the young men of the tribe. There was no doubt in the minds of the young what was expected of them, and it was a literal turning point in their lives. Traditions such as the Jewish practice of Bar Mitzvah and Christian confirmation reflect vestiges of these rites.

Almost all Native American cultures have had rites of passage in some form. In certain cultures, boys were raised with the mothers exclusively until age twelve or so, and then given over to the fathers in ceremony, who then took over full responsibility of raising them to manhood. They were given new names and identities, and although there was much collusion in the process between mother and father, the sons knew nothing about it. The fathers taught the boys the responsibilities of hunting and trapping, fishing and survival, and passed on the history and customs through intensive one-on-one interaction.

Perhaps it is the lack of a traditional rite of passage in the cultural sense that is at the root of our male identity crisis. From a sociological point of view, our rite might well be that we don't have one. That is to say, the concept may be considered to be unnecessary based on our unique "melting pot" tradition. I, however, in looking at the massive failure of relationships in general today, find it difficult to accept that point of view. Even the Japanese, who have become obsessed with the Western way even to the point of rising rates of divorce and juvenile delinquency, still hold on to some very riged understandings about the roles of men and women. I believe that some tradition forming a rite of passage is critical to the bonding in a father/son relationship, even if it is only peeing on a tree together. Without a bonding tradition, I can see no way that we will ever solve the problems we are now facing. Again, if we are to choose a process to experience, it would need to be borrowed either from our traditional religious background, or from the Native American culture. The latter would probably be the Vision Quest.

The Vision Quest is perhaps the most logical and practical form available to us today to participate in. The passing is in reality a change of energy from the feminine family-oriented existence to the masculine responsibility-oriented existence. This is not to say that there is not responsibility inherent in the feminine role, but it is a more passive responsibility.

Once the blending of feminine receptivity into masculine aggression energy has been achieved, the next step is to team that movement up with the right brain to create a vision or goal. To dedicate one's energies to move from point to point, giving emphasis and direction to thought, can help make life passionate, exciting and productive. The father/son relationship can be used as the vehicle to create this movement, and the vision quest is a powerful and exciting tool to use for this purpose. I am not suggesting the pure Native American quest, but one that has been adapted for contemporary use. I have done the "pure" quest, as the Native American does it, and some adapted versions, and found them all to be effective opening experiences. Whichever we choose, the form we pick will be the perfect one for us at that time. In the Native American culture, knowing oneself is of utmost importance. Depending on the tribe, a young man is sent out on his own, usually between the ages of 9 and 14, on what is essentially a survival test-physically, emotionally and spiritually. He will spend anywhere from three to twelve days without food and in some cases without water, or fixed shelter, the goal being to find his vision. That vision may be as simple as a name or recognizing his guide animal, or as soul reaching as seeing one's future work. I am purposely simplifying the details because it is not the specifics that are important but the concept of the male being invested into his own power and purpose. The details of the vision quest will vary from tribe to tribe, but are essentially the same as presented here. Because it is still considered by some to be a sacred rite, it is suggested that interested readers do their own research on the subject. I will say, however, that there are few traditions or rites of passage for the individual that are more meaningful than the vision quest, for getting in touch with the self.

The Bible tells us of the quests of Abraham, Isaac and Jacob, as well as the forty-day quest of Jesus. The intention was spiritual as well as physical and is powerful enough to form an operating foundation of life for many years. I try to do a quest at least once a year, to reinforce, open and re-establish the left brain/right brain cooperative.

Although classically the quest is done alone, it can be done with our sons, in a way that is both bonding and fun, as well as spiritually and intellectually rewarding. On our "Wilderness Journeys, Tours," we set up one of the five days as a vision quest and it is one of the most profound and rewarding experiences of the tour. You can, of course, accomplish this on a self guided basis, but safety is a critical part of the experience and I would not recommend it unless you are well prepared technically. First, set up no intellectual guidelines. Prepare yourself physically and emotionally, but to be fully effective one must go into the quest ready for anything and open to the examination of belief systems. A willingness to accept the truth that to know and love yourself is a prerequisite to knowing and loving your son, (or anyone else,) will put you on the right track. To be effective, it is generally agreed that a minimum of three days is required and five is generally recommended. An extended quest is not actually done on our "Journeys," but the context of it is presented in abbreviated form. The environment can be any wilderness area, but the more rugged and powerful the better. National parks are generally ideal, with the exceptions that they may be too crowded during certain times of the year, and one must be prepared for certain dangers. Aloneness is an important element of the quest. Physical exertion is also a key factor in the successful completion, because you must also extend your physical comfort zone in order to get in touch with your body. Any runner will tell you that the running is only an excuse to get the moment of breakthrough, the connection to that inner most self in the belief system diagram. The body is our living temple to God, the only thing we have with which to experience our lives on this plane of awareness. Our body is a sacred and magnificent manifestation of love with the capacity to reward us with many pleasures and gifts. We were designed as complete units, and none works to its potential if the others are ignored.

Our general abuse of our bodies through poor diets and lack of proper exercise leaves us open to learn much about ourselves by testing our limits. By experiencing these tests with our sons, we will find that what we thought were our limits are only partially so. We will get to experience how our belief systems hold us back from being all we can be, **or anywhere close to it.** As human beings, we are all incredibly powerful and capable packages of energy. We all too often just refuse to believe it. Once we've broken through the belief barrier, we can touch the awareness of our own limitlessness. This breakthrough is our acknowledgment that we, in fact, set up our own limitations. It allows us to see the potentials in our relationships and the power we hold to affect the survival of our planet. Regardless of how hard we try, the old adage "no man is an island" is as true today as ever before. We cannot limit our effectiveness in life by further refusal to take responsibility for our own survival.

The quality of the life we live, now more than ever before in the history of man, is our choice, due to the huge number of options available to us. Many have created lives in which the trade or professional aspects have been dominant. Our personal lives, family and social relationships have been secondary and we fit or shove them into the available time slots left over after work. As social and industrial economies shift, in the natural growth flow, nations having expanded beyond the capacity of their populations to absorb further growth will rapidly become service economies. We are seeing this in our own country on an ever-increasing scale. Looking at the word "service" and its intent, we cannot help but see the importance that the quality of a relationship plays in the process of being in service. One must be in service to self before he can be in service to anyone else.

Survival through the 21st century will require a new look at the energy forces we have discussed. Masculine energy - determined, creative, risk-oriented aggressiveness, is what brought us through the industrialization era. The feminine energy of love and awareness of the self, its effect on our close personal relationships, and the resultant synergistic flow outward, is what will allow America to lead in the future. The vision quest opens us up to the concept of operating from and for a "vision." It can be the first step in recognizing that without a goal or vision, movement is very difficult. Quite simply we must have direction in order to grow, and creating the vision can give us that direction. Our largest and most successful American companies know this, and literally every one of them based its growth on knowing precisely what it wanted to do and in written form followed a dream, a vision, a mission. The IBM mission statement is the backbone of that company. It is present from the board of directors meeting to the entry-level sales training programs. This does not mean that we must plod ahead blindly on a given course, just because we decided that this was what we wanted. The vision should be broad enough to allow flexibility and movement within its attainment. The growth will occur along the path of attainment, and accomplishment of the vision will be its own reward.

For the male there is no closer connection to the world than our sons. We avoid them because we fear them. We fear them because until we know who we are we know we cannot guide them, and are scared to death they will find out and hate us. Our anger at their misdeeds is our anger at ourselves for not being enough and it is not going to change until we collectively say "enough." In that small body looking up to us, reaching out to us, is all the love we will ever need, but until we accept it, it will go nowhere.

*if you don't like your reality, you
must change your beliefs, and thoughts,
and expectations.*

conversations with seth
Watkins

TOOL #15
ROLE MODELING, SELF-LOVE

We have discussed, in other areas, the importance of love of self, self-image and self-esteem. Role modeling is a process by which a person begins to see the picture of himself as an extension of those around him. It can be either a positive picture or a negative one, and it is usually complete by the age of five. Unfortunately, due mainly to the father-absent syndrome, too many of us grow up with an overabundance of negative role modeling. Our images are made up less of how we see ourselves than how we *believe* others see us. That is created by reaction to our world, rather than being in causality. We react negatively because we see ourselves as not being able to reach the standards of the positive role models in our lives. We allow fear to be a dominant force in our lives. Lack of positive self-image moves us to react to being less than we are capable of being. Many of us live our role models through our twenties and thirties, and the challenges to that image generally start to appear seriously during the thirties. On a subconscious level, at least, we begin to notice that by thirty-five or so our healthy, productive life is nearing the probable halfway point, and our mental and experiential conditioning sees the second half as downhill, slower, less productive. The problem lies in the fact that our expectations create our judgments of our reality. We do become what we believe we will become. Unfortunately, fear is a greater force in that direction than positiveness, and because low self-esteem among men is very common, fear has easy access. We must constantly be on the move and consciously creating positive flow. If we just lie back and wait for the universe, or others, to fix us or themselves, the ego moves in with all its protective tools and we buy into the "half over," downhill, negative syndrome. That is one of the primary reasons why so many people in their thirties begin to look outside themselves for ways to get in touch with their inner feelings. We see people looking back to rejected childhood religious experiences, or adopting new spiritual beliefs, seeking professional counseling, looking for new meaning and purpose. These are all fine paths to follow, but none is a substitute for finding that place within in which we know for certain who we are. These side roads in which we seek answers without are the methods of discovery. What we find in the exercise of going without is that we already have our answers within. We also find a great deal of resistance to this whole idea. That is why a vision quest can be so beneficial and dynamic an event in a person's life. Without an effort to discover who we are so that we can love that, we float through our lives becoming victims of our expectations, rather than causal of our experiences.

Our early role models are generally based on fantasy, with images of ourselves creating wonderfully positive pictures of beauty, grace, power and success. Such pictures are reinforced by the advertising industry, TV and even the educational systems. These are wonderful examples for us to start out with, but they are quickly smothered by our perceptions of reality. As a six year old, there was never a moment's doubt in my mind that I could be a better Roy Rogers than Roy, if only I could convince my parents that we could keep a horse in the house. (In a way I suppose I was better off than with todays television hero's, who are primarily bafoons or purveyors of grotesque violence.)

Television does not demand the mind to exercise, and, in fact, reaches the unconscious through a trance state. Radio at least demands concentration and the forming of mental pictures, in fact requiring a rather complex series of brain activities, to facilitate understanding. Preserving these fantasies and the pleasures they bring to us while keeping a level of reality at the same time seems impossible. So, by the teenage years, we have pretty well lost our ability to fantasize and are well grooved into our left brain experiences. Through actions of commitment such as the vision quest and relaxed states of meditation, we can get to re-experience our fantasies in a way that helps to open our right brain contribution to our daily life, and open ourselves up to greater possibilities. We can begin to see ourselves fulfilled, as heroes to ourselves, as adventurous swashbucklers on the wave of life!

At any age or level of experience, we can find someone who has attributes and values worth emulating, and by interpreting these attributes through our own individuality, we apply ever increasing right-brain influence and can advance to new heights of self love and awareness. "Love thyself"... easy words; tough trip, but worth the toll. Self-love is created through self-examination and a recognition that there is only now; that life exists only in this moment; and that you must participate in order to receive its gifts.

MENTORSHIP

Role modeling and self-love are totally integrated and interrelated effects. Boys have no particular exclusivity on the need for role models. Many women and men hold others in a place of awe, who could be considered role models. If the person is a professional, teacher, friend or relative, often he/she fall into the position of mentor, becoming an influential guide. Particularly with men, however, mentors easily can become father replacements, particularly when in the work environment. The mentor relationship can be looked at in many different lights both positively and negatively, but is always father-based. The mentor seeking to share as teacher and the mentee seeking to secure direction from the father never realized. Self-image becomes critical in this kind of interaction because of the high probability of hidden unconscious agendas on the parts of both parties. The higher the level of self-esteem on both sides, the more beneficial such a relationship becomes. The problem is that the concept of mentorship fits most easily the needy and dependent, not the strong and interdependent. Further complicating this potentially beneficial relationship is the old male resistance factor. Many men will resist being helped on any level, believing it a sign of weakness, which exposes their vulnerability, or even worse fear it as a homosexual attraction. Women do not have this complication, technically known as hemophobia, and rarely understand the deep fear men have of it. It again is self esteem based because we don't have definition and control of our masculinity enough to be confident of our heterosexuality. We do not know how to love ourselves enough, and the mentor relationship is a love relationship, which challenges us at every turn.

Mentoring is an important subject for men because it brings up all the issues of the father/son, friend and lover relationships. If you are a man, think about the men who are your "heroes." Could you think of them as mentors? How would you approach such a relationship? Jot down the thoughts that come into your mind about it without judging them. What is it about these men that attracts you? What qualities do they possess that you would like to have? Visualize yourself with these qualities and try to see what kinds of differences it would make in your life. Look at the issues you would have to deal with to get to that place. Now make a second list of those issues, and you will have a list of the key issues for you to work on. Start by relating them to your belief systems. Analyze their structure and then meditate on them by just keeping them in your conscious awareness. Simply the fact that you are allowing them into your conscious thoughts will open the way for healing to take place.

These questions and your efforts to move them to the surface will open access to the right brain. Ask yourself as each thought comes up, "How do I feel about that?" Not "*What do I think*," but "*How do I feel?*" Neuro-Linguistically the word "*feel*" will access the emotional responses you will need to get through the process. To "*think*" about something is a left-brain process, and emotions cannot respond to analytical process. This is why communication is so difficult between men and women. The woman wants to feel the problem and the man wants to figure it out. No communication takes place.

If you find a particular man with whom you feel a mentoring relationship is appropriate, explore it on the basis of mutual benefit. It could be an exciting and lesson filled adventure. One thing is for sure, you cannot help but expand and grow with it. Don't forget, however, that the other person will need to understand, as you do what is going on and be willing to share the experience. It may not be easy; men are not accustomed to these kinds of relationships with other men.

*In speaking of love, remember that
you cannot do it, you cannot will it,
and you cannot demand it. All you can
do is begin to follow a path that you
hope embodies it.*

Bartholomew

TOOL # 16
PASSION

As I meet, work with, and talk to men, I sense several things common to most of us. Most noticeable is the sadness of which I spoke earlier. With the sadness comes a lack of that deep, penetrating, touching energy we call passion. The older we get, the less it seems to be present. We normally think of passion in its sexual context, but that is only one place it shows up. What I have observed is that passion tends to be a constant in our personalities, being represented equally in all ares of our experience at the same level of intensity. This may come as quite a shock to many men, but we don't manufacture passion under the sheets, we bring it in with us. If we don't have it at work, in the supermarket, in the way we are in service to our fellow man, in our political views, then we won't have it in bed.

Passion is a habit, not a printout from the DNA. We first must know that we don't have it, find out why and then find a way to get it back. I say "get it back" because I believe we all come in with a full complement of it. Just watch a hungry baby crying for food. That is natural passion. One of the things the filters filter out with exceptional efficiency is our passion. Look back the list of male attribute by age (page 39). It is the loss of passion that creates these patterns of behavior.

Coming to terms with our maleness is the way to regain that feeling of commitment that leads to setting and achieving our goals. The level of passion we put out is directly related to our degree of commitment, and visa versa. One might say that commitment is measurable by the amount of passion available. Passion is cnergy, and we are in choice about how much of it we allow in. Pure choice. That makes us responsible for it, just like everything else. The loss of passion we see in men by age doesn't have to be that way. It is your choice. The most important thing to know is that passion is consistent across our experience. This is a particularly serious matter as we get older. We lose what we believe is our sexuality, or sexual attraction. If we are still confusing our sexuality with our maleness, there will be greater problems for us. We attain a certain level of social "invisibility" (which women share with us to at least an equal degree). We fail to realize our impact on others, and the passion of our commitments and visions wants to slow down and often just disappears. It is important to remember that at fifty years of age most men can expect to live at least half again their present age. I will soon see that half-century mark myself; I don't know about anyone else, but I'm not about to give up my passion about anything. Part of that passion is my commitment to sharing the beauty and wonder of maleness with anyone who will listen... With passion!

*Those who are mentally and emotionally healthy
are those who have learned to say yes,
when to say no,
and when to say whoopee!*

Willard S. Krabill

TOOL #17
NON WORKABLE RELATIONSHIPS

Who of us has not encountered people deeply into the pain of a non-working relationship, with either their children or spouse and more frequently than not, both? They insist that they've tried everything possible to work out the problems, but a better situation just does not seem to develop. Their comments are always the same, "It just wasn't meant to work." These kinds of relationships can be looked at in a new way: by accepting the premise that all relationships work, but each at different levels. Each human experience we touch in some manner leaves us with lessons learned, if we choose to look. If we are in a relationship that is not working as well as we might like it to, we must ask ourselves why, and listen very carefully to the answers we get. There is no better way to do this than within the quietness of a meditation. Perhaps, on a subconscious level, we don't want it to work any better, to avoid having to accept responsibility for our part in it. Peer group pressure, social or ethnic expectations, may also affect the relationship; ("how would it look to my business associates if this does not work out?") Consider that, given the required amount of intention and commitment, any relationship can be made to work. It is a function of the power given by both parties to the relationship concept, and an agreement on common need, purpose and value.

Now, we are not talking passionate love here, we're talking basic human interactions. You and your fourteen-year-old who suddenly no longer speak the same language. The husband and wife with 25 years together, finding the kids gone and the nest empty, who must now face each other. They may have looked forward to this time for many years, but now that it's really here, suddenly they find it "isn't working anymore," and they opt for separation. Occasionally it will work out for the better. But for the most part, each will grow alone and separate, in ways that might better have been shared. Some find new partners, others just give up, and based on their previous beliefs, live their lives out alone. Abandoned relationships may miss a very special opportunity to capitalize on a full but denied history and depth of shared experience that can never be duplicated. Many will say, "We've been miserable for years and only stayed together for the sake of the kids." If that is really true, it's not a very good reason and it didn't do the kids any good at all. The chances are the kids knew about it all the time, and created neuroses of the same depth and intensity that they would have created had the parents split -

just different ones. A lousy relationship cannot be hidden from anyone, especially our kids. The problem is our tendency to perceive the other person as responsible for our failure to be fully involved in our moment. If we are doing the best we can to be all we can be in each moment, then we will automatically be responsible for our part in the relationship. In a way it's a lot like being bored at a concert or a party. The boredom comes not from some intrinsic value that the event "has," but in our willingness not to be present in the event. We bore ourselves, and we are the only ones who can! Once we accept the responsibility that it is our choice, we must act upon it, and once we act, we create movement. If, as discussed, movement is growth, our relationship is going to grow.

Each of us, of course can only grow for our half of the twosome, and the other half must grow also. What seems to happen is where there is a commitment to the third-party relationship, the other person also will move to complete his or her parts. It may not be easy, but it is a start to a new level of understanding. Part of the responsibility factor is a recognition that each must grow and expand at a rate consistent with his/her own inner self awareness, no expectations allowed. Through unconditional love, we can help our partners move at their own pace and still move at our own rate, not without conflict, but certainly with love. Now it well may be that through unconditional love and allowing another, be it spouse or child, it becomes clear that you simply are growing in different directions. In such a case, splitting up becomes inevitable, and trying to keep it together just prolongs the pain. But in these instances there is a good chance that the separation can be handled in a manner that supports both parties. In effect a third-party relationship is developed around the splitting up, and new parameters are set up. It is amazing what can be accomplished between two human beings when the anger is replaced with compassion.

As I mentioned in the beginning of the book, I have moved back and forth with regularity between the influences of the spouse and offspring relationships, with little differentiation. That is done because I hold no real separation between human reaction based on the type of relationship. If we have created problems with our children, we have created problems with our spouses, and vice versa; it can be counted on. Something else that can be counted on is that the problems all come from the same place. To apply this concept to our children first is easier, because by the time conflict begins to show up as a reaction in the kids, problems have to be at a critical level with the parents, and the history can be a huge blockage. As the father/son relationship begins to thaw, feminine energy will be reated and rub off within the family structure, generating a springboard of trust upon which to build.

In most marital conflicts trust is the issue that comes up first. It may look like, and be called, many other things, such as finances, time, attention, other priorities, etc., but the foundation usually lies in trust. Trust, however, is not the basic issue, but the result of low self-esteem. So when we do not trust a particular person it is usually because our own self-esteem is somehow threatened by that person. We need to go to our own issues about what we see in that other person that is reflecting the mistrust. Through the concept of mirroring our reactions, it can be seen that usually the trust issue is with ourselves, not the other person. Much conflict is introduced into our lives by our not being able to trust that we are big enough to handle our challenges. Not trusting that we are capable of dealing with what we perceive as relationships that are not working. The experience gained at the father/son level allows us to expand successes upward through the nuclear family, and outward into society. Working relationships equal a working planet. Taking responsibility for the moment, and operating from a position of unconditional love and respect for another human being's right to grow at his/her own pace are the keys. Following these keys, one should never again experience an unworkable relationship, or be without the tools to move it to whatever level chosen. Not a manipulative process; it is, rather, an allowing process that ends up in free choice and free will.

Consider, if you will, another concept - if you are in a relationship that you feel isn't working, it is because that is the way you want it! Many may be in a state of high resistance to that one. I became exposed to this concept several years ago in a relationships course, and have worked with it ever since. I have found that although not always readily seen, this truth underlies most of our quests for self-understanding. On a motivational level, in fact, consider the possibility that in any part of our lives, we generally have exactly what we want, or we wouldn't have it. Human will and the resultant capacity to manifest what we truly want, are an astounding power. This concept was eloquently explained in 1949 by Napoleon Hill in his book "*Think and Grow Rich*" and in the 1950's by Dr. Norman Vincent Peale, in his "*Power of Positive Thinking*." It has been expanded upon and viewed from as many different angles as one can imagine, but remains essentially the same. It has been supported by all religious points of view, all of the world's greatest and most successful people. It has been called "creative manifestation," "positive attitude," "creative selling," and dozens of other labels. This belief in one's own self is empowered as *the* great motivating force in every success-oriented book ever written, and is given credit by almost every success story ever told. Easier in free societies, of course, but even under severe political and social constraints, open observation will reveal the determined, goal-oriented human spirit can attract into it exactly that which it needs to survive. In higher-developed, free societies, the very substance of survival and continuance is based on the ability to create what we want in our lives. If you've created conditions that you *believe* are other than what you truly want, take a good look at this concept.

Start with your definition of the word "want." Spend some time with your inner self, examining the issues at stake. If your relationship with your son is not what you "want," ask what it is that you may be getting from the interaction as it exists. Believe it or not, there is always a payoff. You may be subconsciously fulfilling a role model pattern set up in your early years with your own father. If your early relationship with him was not a good one, are you assuming the responsibility and resultant guilt? Having a poor connection with your son may be your payback for that guilt trip. Or it could be the fear of discovery that we talked about earlier. I have found that many men appear to be terrified that their sons will find out who they *really* are, and will hate them for it. This is baseline low self esteem at work.

If the issue is with a spouse, it just as easily could be the old "trust" issue. If you have self-worth issues with which to deal, and who doesn't, you also have self-trust issues. Without trust in yourself, again as with love, there cannot be trust in anyone else. Failure to trust closes the free space around us and those closest to us. Without free space, we suffocate. Lack of trust restricts both our growth and our ability to manifest what we truly want. It creates jealousies, anger and resentment, all non-productive conditions.

Through the application of unconditional love, we can look in-depth at what we have, without blame and the pain of guilt. By taking responsibility for our results, we can usually see what we have *is* what we want. Because there is only this moment, we can have something very different in the next moment, if, through commitment, we chose it to be so. Again the key to seeing the positive side of our troubles is knowing that we are not our results. Results are only relative measures of what we are creating in the moment we are in. By getting in touch with our ability to manifest creatively, a flow of understanding and compassion will result, expanding the feminine energy flow, and adding to our balance. Balanced lives work better than unbalanced lives. These often are not easy concepts to accept. If you're up for a risk, invest two refrigerator door, *"What I've got is what I want."* If, after two weeks of repeating this phrase, you haven't moved in your belief systems about the results you've created in your life, you'll see how powerful your resistance to change is. More than likely you will get a glimpse of the possibilities that exist for you.

I hope you've guessed by now that what all this leads up to is the conclusion that there is no such thing as relationships that are non-workable. If a relationship is not what you believe you'd like it to be, it is simply because somewhere along the line both parties have failed to communicate to each other what it is that they want from the relationship.

Two things are required of you to make the concept of self-manifestation work in your life and in your relationships:

1.Knowing what you want.

2. Communicating it.

*Nothing is as far away as
one minute ago.*

unknown

TOOL # 18
FORGIVENESS

During my college years, I took some basic behavioral psychology courses and became fascinated with aspects of cause and effect in human responses. In my training as an industrial designer, knowing what motivated people to buy or not buy certain shapes, colors, textures, etc., was important. The success or failure of any product can hinge on such factors. In subsequent study and working experience, I became quite knowledgeable in this area and came to some interesting conclusions. One is that our environment influences us to a much greater degree than we are generally aware. Another is that the subconscious acts as one big closet that continues collecting our "stuff" as the years go by, and the more full the subconscious becomes the more it controls our life responses. In my late thirties, I ran into a young psychologist, who, in the course of counseling my wife and me, dragged all our "stuff" from our closets, under very painful circumstances. He listened with an almost bored attention to our stories, and then said quite simply, "So that's your story? Fine. Now what are you going to do about it?" At the time I wasn't very impressed, because at $50 an hour, quite frankly I wanted more reinforcement about what a lousy childhood I'd had, or at least confirmation about how wrong my wife was. As time went by, however, I began to see the wisdom in his remark, and it strikes me that it fits perfectly in the context of this discussion. Many of us spend a good portion of our lives in pain, guilt and even terror, of childhood events, wounds long ago forgotten by the conscious memory, or stuffed down inside, where it is easy to ignore, but always present subconsciously. These hidden things can have enormous control over our conscious awareness, without our being at all cognizant. We learn to see ourselves as images of our experiences, rather than masters of our destiny. The psychologist's remark, "Now what are you going to do about it?" breaks down further to *"So what?"* So our father beat us, or our parents deserted us, or our brother got all the attention, or whatever your story is. So what? What are you going to do with the rest of your life? The options seem clear enough, and the wisdom to see them is within us.

We are exposed day in and day out to sayings and quotes that deal with the same subject matter: *"Today is the first day of the rest of your life";" If it is to be, it's up to me";" I am my own destiny";* we could go on for pages, but it is our recognition of the meaning behind these sayings that will get us moving. Of all the sayings I've heard and read, one that hits home for me is: *"There's no one out there."* What it means to me is a reinforcement of the mirror concept. All those bodies out there are only mirror reflections of ourselves. We can, if we choose to look, see ourselves in those we blame for our misfortunes and incompleteness, or with whom we have conflict. We tend to like and dislike those qualities in others that we like and dislike in ourselves. Test it out with your kids. Those tendencies that your son displays that drive you up a wall will most often be those qualities that you reject as being "faults" in your own success story, either consciously or subconsciously.

In the process of looking at our lives, we can see others in the light of their own experiences, rather than our viewpoint of "how it should have been." We also get an opportunity to forgive and let go of blame, guilt and pain. None of these "beat me ups" really exists outside of the mind, and therefore serves no purpose in holding onto. To release, we must first learn to forgive.

The forgiving process brings feminine energy into our being. By forgiving past transgressions against us, we express our love outward. By expressing love outward we automatically express it inward. The getting is in the giving. By zapping those who may have hurt us in attempting to love us, with a little love and forgiveness, and recognizing that there, but for time and space go we, we can let go, a bit at a time, of pain, guilt and anger. Once we have emptied the space those emotions filled, we have room for creative, positive growth. Take a look at your own parents from a role-model point of view. The chances are excellent that you are with your children, very much as your parents were with you. It's just the way we do it, because of the importance role-modeling plays on our subconscious patterning. To forgive our parents for what we interpret as inappropriate behavior on their parts is a major step to realization of our wholeness.

Whether your parents are alive or not, you can deal with past transgressions, because in truth, the transgressions are held in your consciousness, not theirs. Generally parents truly do love their children, whatever it may look like to the child. The natural process of parental responsibility is too powerful and instinctively ingrown into our systems to deny. Our failures (if we choose to look at them in that way) in parental responsibilities is in our ability to cope and communicate. We all share this common human weakness in varying degrees, and it makes no more sense to blame our parents for their failures than it does to blame ourselves for ours. We are just doing the best we can, and so were they. If we allow ourselves the power of coming from unconditional love and surrender, we can experience the reality of: *"that that was, was; that that is, is."* And it can never be any different. You can go to your parents in your imagination and heal many wounds. Once you've healed those, you can start on the ones you've created. It's not right, it's not wrong, it just is. The same is true of self love. You cannot love another if you cannot love yourself first. You cannot heal the wounds you've created until you heal the wounds inflicted upon you. Looking backwards will not change the reality of your experience, but it can alter its effect on your now. Know that whatever your hard and firm belief systems want you to accept as truth, we humans *always* do what we believe to be best at the moment we do it, or we quite simply wouldn't do it. Again, this is a concept that many would argue. The logic behind it however, is solid. Even when we are motivated by cases of self destruction, we believe in the moment that what we are doing will solve our problems. Many look back on acts that did not achieve their goals as "failure." It is certainly more helpful to look at them as lessons, because our mind's eye sees failure as negative and lessons as positive. The transgressions and errors of judgment we feel our parents made were the right course of action for them, at that moment in time, as were ours. There is no right or wrong about it, there's just *"so what?"* *Now, what are you going to do with the rest of your life?* Our ability to effect changes and make a difference in the lives of others is limited by our willingness be part of the difference. Take your share of that responsibility seriously. You alone can stop the destruction of the planet. There really is no one else out there.

Try a little meditation. Sit quietly, go inside to your own greatness and power, and talk gently to those with whom you carry conflict and anger. Be prepared to cry a little, or a lot, and bring up whatever is there for you emotionally. The ability of release through crying is why we cry, and one of the truly great human experiences. No other two-legged, four-legged, winged or crawling creature can do that. No other needs to. The need is to forgive, not necessarily to forget. The lessons are all valuable. Offer unconditional love, compassion, and understanding for the conditions present at the time of the transgression, and then let go. You will be able to free yourself a little more of unneeded burdens, and create even more space to be filled by light from the right brain, and who knows where else.

Keep in mind the possibility that your secret to self-discovery lies in the father relationship. The key to that relationship lies in forgiveness. Forgiving Dad for not living up to our expectations, forgiving ourselves, for judging him through those expectations, and learning to see him through clean filters. Dad issues are symbolic in two major ways. First, we must deal with those emotional conflicts of which these pages are full. Second is the relationship between the life father and God The Father. God The Father is the spirit within that connects us to all things in the universe. Acceptance of one is dependent on our ability to accept the other. We now come full circle in the importance of the spiritual self. As the graphic below shows we are made up of mind, body and spirit. We cannot exist without all three and life is a process of seeking balance of the three segments. To reach forgiveness and accept the life father and the God The Father is a great step to obtaining this balance.

FATHER EXERCISE

The following questions are designed to open the spirit and access the emotions. It is important to do this exercise with the specific intent to allow your feeling to come forth. Write your answers in a notebook that you can keep for further reference. It is best to find a quiet place, or if it is comfortable for you to do so, have a loved one read them to you. Either way don't give up on them; just say or write whatever comes into your mind. If you think at first a particular question is not relevant to your case, just make up an answer, but answer them all. Each answer will stir an emotional response, and it is through this emotion that your work will be done.

The following are written assuming the father is either not living or non-resident. If your father is living and accessible, put the frame of reference in the present.

What I got from my father was:
What I did not get from my father was:
What I wanted most from my father was:
What my father wanted me to know about him was:
What my father did not want me to know about him was:
What my father never told me was:
What my father wanted me to know about him and my mother was:
If he could have written his own epitaph, it would have said:
Dad, I felt hurt by you the most when:
Dad, I loved you the most when:

Read the answers over, and know that every one is a truth in your life. The answers reflect what you wanted from him, and what you want from your son, daughter, spouse etc. We are all the same: fathers, sons, friends or lovers. We see the reflection in our wives and daughters and all those we come in contact with. In these responses lie the definition of who we are, and it cries to be shared. Only you can do it. There is much strength and beauty in those answers. Keep the list and the responses close by so that they are not forgotten. If your Dad is not living, it is absolutely OK to talk to your father at any time you wish, and settle any undone business with him.

Very often these questions will bring up feelings of strong anger. Express that anger...tell him how angry you are and why. Beat on a pillow if you must to express your feelings. Do what-ever it takes to *tell* him how you *feel*.

If he is alive, know that he's done the best he could do, and that he needs to be acknowledged for that. It is a very strong probability that your father does not know how to receive very well. It kind of comes with the territory, but his need to be appreciated is deep and just as important as yours. The harder it is for you to reach out, the more you need to do it, and the more powerful will be the results. If it is your son with whom you have the greatest passion, visualize him answering the questions, and listen to the answers. You will know everything you need to know to create what you want. From the standpoint of your own emotional health and the success of your relationships, this could be the most important exercise of your life.

Once again, I particularly welcome reader's comments on this section.

*The beauty and the power and the
joy in life is not in what happens,
it is in the motion, in the movement,
in the constant changing of all that
happens.*

Bartholomew

TOOL #19
WHAT DO YOU WANT?

Not too many years ago our "wants" had very little to do with how we lived. As we discussed earlier, mankind has been into basic survival for most of history, and what he wanted most was to find the least painless path to tomorrow, and there perhaps, salvation, whatever that may be. There are, in fact, many people who still live their lives this way, but for the most part, we have come a very long way. As the nature of man and his societies, particularly "free" societies, began to change, one of the first things we discovered was our potentials. We began to exercise these gifts in a way that has brought us to the greatest turning point in our earthbound development since the control of fire. Our potentials are being explored in every direction imaginable, and we are just beginning to see the extent of our possibilities as a creative universal force. But we are also dangerously close to annihilating our species, and all others along with us. The ultimate result of this twentieth-century organized madness is simply a result of asking the question, *"What do you want?"*

The truth is, we can never catch up to our potentials. We are simply moving too fast and our potentials are increasing exponentially to our ability to cope with them. To fight that is suicide. We must learn to accept ourselves as we are, do the best we can in every moment to be the most we can be, and let go of the stress and tension that result from trying to be everything to everyone. I once read a report by a think tank analyst estimating that on a worldwide basis we double the amount of new information being created every twenty minutes. There is no way even to get it in all the computers, much less keep up with it on an individual basis. Let's face it, it's hopeless. Why waste our lives trying for the impossible, when the possible is at our fingertips? It is only a matter of definition.

Perhaps the most often asked question in our populace today, "What do you want?" also creates the most frustration. Finding out what you want can be most difficult and time-consuming. The older you are the more time you've had to become confused and defused (and the cloudier the ultimate picture) but the degree of difficulty actually has no relationship to age.

There are as many different processes available to gain clarity about what you want as there are things to want. Consider the following few: prayer, insight and awareness trainings, spiritual pursuits, the ministry, meditation, seminars, retreats, and each with many sub-directions. Each deals with ways to expand the conscious understanding of who we are and why we are here, but they all require the same simple, basic action of introspection. On our father/son journeys, we get a chance to look at what we want in several different ways through "experiential communication." What comes into sharp focus through any of these programs, is that we all seem to want the same personal things, once we get past the cars, boats and bigger houses.

What we want can generally be divided into two fundamental classifications: one is **emotional,** sometimes including and being confused with spiritual needs, particularly when one is "stuck" looking outside oneself for one's answers. The other is **material,**- all the "stuff" used to define the quality of our survival. A most beneficial way to attempt the process of discovery is to look not at the destination, the specific thing you want, but at the journey, because if it is measurable results that you need to have, that is where they exist.

Your approach, of course, is going to be a little different in searching for the "grail" than will be the next person's. The following exercise is one option proven successful in opening up the locked chest of possibilities for many. Find a notebook and put the following headings on successive pages:

1.Ten things I would like to have in my life.
2.Ten things I would like not to have in my life.
3.Ten people whom I would like to know I love them.
4.Ten people whom I would like to know love me.
5.Ten reasons why I believe the results I've projected in
     the questions above don't exist in my life now.

Women generally have little problem with this exercise. Most men go through agony with it, but I have not yet met the person who couldn't answer all the above questions. It is matter of how much risk we are willing to take to look at something we might not want to see.

Now you've had a chance to put into writing what you believe you want in your life, and why you believe you have not achieved it. Two things have just happened. First, you've had an opportunity to see physically, what you want, and in the process, make certain value judgments about them. Second, you have made some acknowledgments on a subconscious level. The first step to commitment is acknowledgment of the *need for action*. The first step to growth is commitment *to* action, so your growth process already has begun. - See how easy it is? - Now, let's take a close look at the last question on the list. The reason you believe that what you want does not exist in your life will tell you much about why it doesn't manifest. Often, self-image is the "culprit."

Take the last list and subdivide it into two more lists, labeling them "wants" and "needs." Take your time in doing this and really evaluate what you define as those things you want vs. those things you truly need. Your "needs" list should be very short. *Anything beyond air, food and water is excessive.* A need is only that which we require to maintain our minimum level of survival. Our "wants" determine the quality of that survival. So, if you accept this definition, everything else is a want. Wants are always subject to change, and anything subject to change is an element of choice. Once we accept that, it is clear that if we do not accept responsibility for making our own choices in our lives, others will make them for us. The reason we so often feel we are "victims" is that we let others make our choices for us.

We avoid taking responsibility for our actions, and allow others to absorb us in their power. If our relationships are not what we would like them to be, it is easily seen that it is because that's the way we want it. We want it that way because it is easier than finding out what we *really* want and taking responsibility for creating it.

Once you've done your lists, discuss them with those you love and whose lives are intertwined with yours. Have them do their own lists and discuss them. By knowing and expressing what you want and what they want, you will have a clear (but not necessarily easy) path to the creation of those things. Positive thought creates positive action. The process is called the law of the Universe, *"That which you put out, you get back,"* or as the Native American would say, *"That which goes around, comes around".* Some call it spiritual law, "Speak to the Lord, and he will hear"; Others see it as simple physical manifestation, creating conscious awareness through experiential sharing. I believe it is all of these and perhaps more. What I know is, it works. What I also know is that if we don't know what we want, we haven't worked hard enough to find out. The problem is that *until you find out what you want, nothing positive is going to happen.*

Many are easily frightened into non-expansion because of the risk involved. Let's face it, what is involved here is we may find out what we have is not what we want, and then what do we do? Quite simply, the only thing we can do is take full responsibility. Many of us sit in jobs of high responsibility, and are extremely capable in our chosen fields of work, yet refuse to accept the same level of accountability to allow our close relationships to work. Your job guidelines are well defined and you are required to perform to certain levels of competence.

These guidelines are set on certain objectives and goals that constitute the "wants or needs" of the job. You can do the same thing in your personal life with these lists. If you still don't know what you want, don't beat yourself up about it, just list the things you "think" you want. *Life is about the process and not the result.*

The process will still work. Because this book is about relationships, and you're reading it, a safe assumption is that at or near the top of your list of things you want in your life is either a prime relationship or a more effective one with your wife or son. If you *really* want that to happen, it will. All you need to do is risk a little. Participate in their lives, and respect their ground rules. Share your moments with them. Work with them in a way that they understand you want to be with them, in ways that work for all of you. Be in their moments with them. Once they begin to share their feelings about things beyond anger and expectations, you will have created an opening to learn great things. You also might find that they are pretty incredible people.

*Very little is needed to make
a happy life. It is all within
yourself, in your way of thinking.*

Marcus Aurelius

TOOL# 20
TRUST

In each of the areas we've discussed, one factor controls our ability to make them work. Our own self-image. Called self-esteem, ego, self-confidence or a multitude of other things, it probably is a combination of whatever we believe it to be, but it boils down to simply a matter of how well we trust ourselves. Trust has become a major issue of the twentieth century, so no wonder it shows up in how we view ourselves. I can't think of a single country that completely trusts the word of another. Even those countries called Allies require treaties to define common interests, not to mention how we operate with those countries we see as enemies. Our entire operating environment is based on distrust. Wherever we go, whatever we do, we are always within the touch of some measure designed to ensure our mode of transaction, so that trust doesn't even have to enter into the picture. We "protect" our kids, so that they will not have to trust their own strength, and then wonder why they can't be trusted. We overtly control our relationships, because we are not willing to trust that those we love will love us back if we don't control them. The phrase *"In God we Trust"* is emblazoned throughout our government and legal system, but we **operate** from, *"but just in case!"* Love without trust is love headed for trouble. If we will not trust someone to be whatever and whoever they feel they must be, our love is then conditional.

Unconditional love, which is love that truly serves all participants, is based, then, on trust. Trusting ourselves is dependent on trusting our intuition, or inner knowing. It is also having the willingness to act on something just because it "feels" right. To take a risk that the unknown is only the unknown, with neither positive nor negative attributes attached.

Operating in the moment can help get us to that point, by preventing our getting caught up in all the left-brain intellectual activity that creates distrust. If we trust that the results of each moment can be handled in the next moment, we can open up our limited self image in vast ways. Trust is a quality closely tied in to our old friend perfection. The person operating from a place of perfection never can allow himself to trust anyone fully. That is because perfection leaves no room for error, and in order to trust another at any level, we must acknowledge their right to a point of view different from ours. That difference can be easily perceived as error, or being wrong, when viewed by the perfectionist.

The perfectionist, however, need not lower his goals in life. The truth is that we are who we are, and that really doesn't change much, no matter how many seminars and courses we take. What we can change is the heaviness and rigidity with which we hold our views, and the effect we have on those around us as we pass their way. The joy in life is inherent in the journey. We are all going to the same place in the end. Does it really matter whether we subscribe to the belief that the soul reincarnates for further lessons to be learned, or that we have one shot either to sit by the side of God, or sweat out eternity in purgatory? What is inarguable as reality on this life plane is that we are born, we live and we die, in our bodies. Whatever may happen to our universal essence after that is a direct result of the journey in body. Even if nothing at all happens, if this earth existence is just one big lottery with no God or esoteric universal mind, it is still all we've got. Even if, as some quantum physicists would have us believe, there is no reality at all, outside our perception, then we still have our perception to live through! If we miss the opportunity to love and trust our own beautiful essence, and that of those we beget, we will have lost our inheritance.

Self-image is a highly complex part of our psyche, affected by many factors. But more than any other, self-image is vulnerable to change because it is what we believe it to be, and we can change those belief systems at will. That vulnerability is also why our image can be affected so easily by outside factors. Most of the world's great religions give us the opportunity to forgive our transgressions, but modern religions allows us to give the responsibility away, along with the guilt. The earth plane requires us to handle our forgiveness within, by seeing ourselves as sacred and a part of the God energy manifest in life form. We need to see ourselves in the wonder and perfection of the moment that each of is in. As discussed, meditation is a wonderful tool to get in touch with our images and realities. Quieting the mind and just being has a divine effect, allowing our God self to express itself. The more you meditate, the faster the visualizations will occur, because as you see yourself is how others will see you. See yourself as negative, dull and always on the sidelines, and that is exactly how others will see you. See yourself as positive, accepting problems and looking for the opportunity they bring, and as bringing positive energy to others, and you will be amazed at how your relationships will expand. We all want to be with and be like those who create positive motion in their lives, because that's where the fun and success are. It's hard to beat fun and success, and it need not be a choice.

No faster way to create self-image repair and awareness has been found than the old eye contact routine. To look people in the eye is a form of recognition that they are important. Next time you are in a busy fast-food restaurant, notice that the counter people will rarely "look" at you, much less allow eye-to-eye contact. There may well be a number of reasons for this reaction, but chances are a big one is that they are caught up in the activity of the moment, and that you, as a human being, are just not present for them. But notice what the reaction is if you can create eye contact. Suddenly, all your conscious thoughts become engaged with that person. It's as if the eyes are meant to allow yourself out and others in. This is done on more than a subconscious level by all of us. We get a pretty accurate reading on how people feel about themselves by the extent and degree of how they make eye contact. Don't forget, of course, that they are doing the same with you. Make it a game, and you'll not only have a lot of fun, but you'll make a difference in other people's lives. A word of warning, however: don't go around staring at people. Those who are very insecure or who hold little self-esteem can be literally panicked by someone staring at them. Notice also your own comfort level.

Many Americans raised in urban areas enter into adult life with huge trust issues. We've learned to lock our houses and cars for fear of theft. We load up on insurance of all kinds. We protect our wallets and purses like life itself, as though we were our wallets or purses. The security industry is one of the fastest-growing in the country. Our national babysitter, TV, has taught us every foul and deceitful trick imaginable. The folks dreaming them up would collectively fill all the nation's jail cells, if they were actually to perpetrate their crimes themselves. Instead we pay them millions to show us how or how not to commit these crimes ourselves. No wonder we don't trust anyone.

Again, the Vietnam War must be viewed as a principal contributing and reinforcing factor to this national disaster. An entire generation of males grew up in an era when their lives were literally on the line over their choice about what and whom they were willing to trust, and what they discovered was that there was no one who could be believed. Because this distrust shook the very foundation of our country, it shook the support structure of our kids. Trust is essential to the quality of survival, because we can't commit to something we do not see as valid. And without commitment there is no movement. If you do not trust that you are capable of doing whatever is required to make your relationship with your son the best it can be, the result will be exactly what you believe you're capable of. Trust, and I'm sure you've already guessed it, is just another form of belief.

We must believe in ourselves, because if we don't, no one else can. Another's experience of you is all they get to believe about you. By knowing and accepting that each of us is divine and sacred, we put the same trust in ourselves, as we do in God, for, depending on one's point of view, we are either made in his image, or are the same. Not to believe in God's potential is not to believe in ourselves. Keep your power! It's yours, you were born with it. Don't give it up to a guru who already has more than he needs. The true guru doesn't want your power. Stay with your power. Get into it. Be it. Self-love and self-trust cannot be attained overnight, and there will be many wrong turns and ego traps along the path. But if you can find out what you want, and trust that it can be yours, you'll find the journey will change many things in your life. Going back to our discussion of the vision quest to build a simple equation, the vision quest creates the space for our vision of who we are, to become real. That vision allows motivation to build the self-image. To put it into reverse terms, *lack of vision = lack of self-motivation = lack of self-image.*

*Individual and species survival
means increasing our tolerance,
our patience, our understanding,
so that we do not continue to
drive ourselves crazy when people
or situations are not the way we
want them to be.*

The Hundredth Monkey

TOOL #21
THE GIFT WE SHARE

Each day that comes to us brings many learning opportunities. Each new dawn has its surprises and its gifts, and each of us faces them in differing ways. A lot of us are frightened, some literally scared to death, and many others just do not get involved. None of the above is a good place to be. We all can find a place of better personal balance at most times in our lives, and in our perception of our world. No radical new points of view, no nationalistic or political revolutions are required. Just becoming involved in our relationships as though they mattered, and learning, or at least, running our lives in the belief that every human has a right to his own belief system, his own space, is all that is necessary.

Negative judgments of these rights are what causes our unhappiness, wars, divorces, kids on drugs, dropouts and most of the world's ills. Will living in the positive, aware moment of acceptance give you happiness forever? Not very likely. The ups and downs, the ins and outs are all part of the lessons we have to learn. To live truly in the belief that life can or should be blissful at every moment is living in the world of perfection and denial. A life with no problems is a life with no opportunity. No knowledge of truth is possible without deceit, no awareness of light without dark, no acceptance of self without doubt. The Yin and Yang of the universe enriches us. The total balance of all energy, good and bad. We get to a point of understanding that all things come to us (either from within, or what we perceive to be without) as gifts. Acceptance of the process allows the gifts to find us.

Allow your sons the right to their own truth. It may not look like your truth, but if it is truth to them, it is Truth. Your respect of that, along with your unconditional love in spite of it, is what will create a bonding with him that will be rich, rewarding and stabilizing. Will it be perfect? Quite probably not. Do you need to stop discipline? Absolutely not. Will he respond? He's human; that is his choice.

The relationship between the student and the teacher is without fixed definitions, but "sharing" certainly must be included. Nothing can be taught unless a student is willing to learn, and in the learning, the student teaches the teacher. Where both students and teachers run into problems is when one or both see their responsibilities in fixed terms, rather than as a sharing of experiences in motion. The teacher who often approaches his or her task from a position of authority or superior status cuts a narrow and difficult path. A true student-teacher working relationship should be one based on a sharing of ideas and thoughts, with both parties coming from a place of learning. One person cannot share fully unless the other is willing to accept.

The degree to which one is willing to accept anyone else sharing is the degree to which the learning potential can be measured. We tend to see students and teachers in stereotypical images, having to do with schools, trainings, etc. In truth, we are all teachers and students, and the real classroom is the instant in time we call life. There is a saying, that we teach others that which *we* need most to learn ourselves. Again, the concept is seeing all other beings as mirror images of ourselves. This process of sharing thoughts and acquired knowledge is the essence of relationship. If we can keep our conscious mind attuned to this concept and operate from a place of sharing, rather than authority, we can positively affect our relationships immediately and with minimal conflict. Sharing feelings, knowledge and intuitive understanding is really all there is to do in the human experience. Our task, if we are to survive, is to learn to share with unconditional love and surrender the idea that the teaching *is* the learning, and that the process of living *is* life, not the result of our accomplishments.

To do this effectively, most of us have a critical need to deal with an acquired desire to be right. This is a particularly dominant factor with men, because of our confused state of our masculinity. To be wrong is to be vulnerable. Being right is being out of touch with our interreaction to others. Being right comes from allowing our left-brain-oriented ego to control our lives, rather than operating from a balance in which the ego serves to give us options of choice (rather than making the choice for us). For many of us, being right is the single most powerful motivating force in our lives. We will literally beat ourselves to death to prove how right we are about our misfortunes in life. Rather than take our full share of responsibility for the messes we get ourselves into, we continue them, in order to be right about how lousy our life is. If our parents continually berated us for being stupid or clumsy, or "a pain in the ass," we became convinced that they were right, and grew up believing we were those things, because to believe any differently would make us wrong, based on what we were told. *And we can't stand to be wrong! The simple truth as it applies to our lives is, we can be right, or, we can have a relationship.*

Truly sharing oneself requires accepting the possibility that our belief about anything, no matter how deeply ingrained, may not sit well with someone else, like our kids, for instance. Allowing oneself to be open to give loved ones the opportunity to be right, and the space to be wrong, as a learning process, automatically will give you the same opportunity. Watch a pair of lawyers doing battle with each other. Often this can be an example of being right carried to the absolute extreme. Lawyers are so invested in their point of view of being right that they will protect that position with their reputations. To be wrong is to lose, and to lose is the dismal depths of despair, depression, and tragedy, not to mention how wrong everybody else was. I have no particular bone to pick with lawyers; they serve a necessary function in our system. I merely use them as an example to help us look at how we operate about being right in our lives. Righteousness comes from being judgmental, and judgmentalism has a nasty habit of getting us into deep trouble. Just ask the salesman who made a judgment about a client not being able to afford his product - then watched as his competitor walked in and made the sale! Making judgments is an inevitable result of being human. *Making or having judgments is not the problem, it's allowing the judgments to become belief systems that run our lives, that creates havoc.* If we allow ourselves the opportunity to have a judgment, acknowledge the fact that we have it, put it aside, and then live in the actual experience, we might discover some new and interesting possibilities. The next time you meet someone about whom you have a negative judgment, go into your risk mode. Create an opportunity to be with them in a friendly way, ignoring your judgment, and experience them and yourself in the interaction.

Finding out the way a person speaks, dresses or wears his or her hair has nothing to do with who they are can be an extremely enlightening experience. "One can be right, or one can have a relationship." That phrase is a belief. It may, or may not, be "right." But the next time you find yourself in a verbal, emotional battle with anyone, bring that phrase up into your consciousness, and see where you stand with it in the moment. This phrase may become one of your best friends.

Many wonderful things are going on in our world today. Our understanding of them is based on our willingness to share and recognize the rights of others to exist. Humanitarian programs such as "Hands Across America," "Children for Peace," "Heart to Heart," Famine Relief Fund raisers, and many others all have essentially the same goal - reaching out from the heart to connect with others in support of their right to exist, on their own terms. Sooner or later, people who represent the world's governments will have to take a look at their own responsibility level, outside of their egos and political ramifications, and one by one, the immense and sometimes seemingly impossible problems of world peace will be faced and dealt with on a workable level. There simply are no alternatives to survival. The solution starts in our own families. The next time you need to confront your son about the use of drugs, denial, lying or any other self-abusive reaction, treat it as a reaction to stimuli, rather than a singular, spontaneously induced event. Don't throw up your hands in abandonment and apply unjust punitive measures because of your anger and frustration. Giving up not only continues the agony, but it will tell him of your unwillingness to stretch for him. Know he is reacting to conditional limitations, negative environmental pressures, role-model failures, and tons of misunderstandings that have created powerful negative belief systems. It's not your fault, or his fault, or anybody's fault. It just is the way it is, but it does not have to continue that way. The choice is yours. Stretch out, risk, reach out to him. You don't need to plan or "know" how or what to say. Just come to him from love, and the words will be there. The heart knows what needs to be said.

As we have seen, studies have indicated that as much as 90 percent of our personal communication comes from sources other than our words. The heart also knows how to listen, and the language is more than words. Come from your heart, and your son will understand that you care and that you care that he cares. Then you and he both can go out into the world and share your love and caring.

...ah, what a beautiful day to die.

Native American saying

TOOL #22
SURRENDER

The subject of surrender is most fitting for the final chapter of this book, for the process of surrender allows the past to be done and the future to become. Through this process we learn to let go of belief systems holding us back from fulfilling our potential. It is the tough part, to be sure, and it is why being one with nature is so important.

During the writing of this book I have visited many wonderful and inspiring places. The deserts and mountains of California, Arizona and New Mexico. I have sat on the top of 10,000-foot peaks and at the bottom of the world in the Grand Canyon. Each, in its own way, in its own magnificent agelessness and unlimitedness, the ultimate surrender. These moments with Mother Earth serve to connect us with what we want more quickly and clearly than any other experience. The effect on the psyche is almost hypnotic, but somehow our judgment becomes simplified and "laser direct" through the magic of the land's energy.

If you have "listened" as you read these chapters, you now have a foundation of ideas that can help make the changes in your life what will bring you the results you want. You also know you had them before you read this book. The point is - are you willing to be responsible for making a difference in the world? Not to save it, or even save a part of it, just to make a difference, in your life. Now comes your commitment level. Surrendering to the possibility that what worked for you yesterday is no longer important at all. Let it go. Let the pains and arguments, disappointments and ego conflicts melt away in the new sunlight of each day, and forget them. Treat each new moment as the last one you may ever have, and fill it with love and positive energy. Surrender to the possibility that your children, spouses, friends and lovers have as much right, and, in fact, the responsibility, to be who they are, as you have to be who you are. Surrender to the possibility that you can have it all. Surrender to the possibility that we are here to learn our lessons and that we choose freely the extent to which we learn them. Surrender to the possibility that no matter what the conditions, there is no generic right or wrong in any action. There is only action, and rightness or wrongness comes as a result of what we believe. Surrender to the knowing that love creates, love moves, love is, and that negative action, dishonesty, lust, greed and non-commitment, create havoc in the human condition.

Work with your sons. Help them to know that these same choices exist for them, and the integrity with which they exercise those choices will determine how closely they come to finding and getting what that want. Allow them the freedom that comes from realizing the only perfection that exists in the universe is in each moment of life itself, and that to expect perfection from human relationships is a guaranteed setup for disaster.

Would you like to see your children have the opportunity to live a life without wars, without starvation, without sacrifice of human life, with less crime and violence, with promise for the future, relationships that work to mutual advantage, and commitments that are kept? Then spend some time with the ideas presented here. There are no quick, easy, free rides to nirvana. But there is an ever-increasing number of opportunities to help handle the transition to peace that must come. The opportunity is with us now in the form of books, seminars, trainings and an endless progression of thoughts. You are the key - your taking responsibility for having what you want in your life, and making the commitment to create it. Nothing different will happen until you do.

I truly hope that what I have been fortunate enough to be able to share with you can help the fathers and sons, mothers and daughters, husbands and wives, to make life a little more fun. If this book serves only to touch a few, who are able to open their hearts and minds to other possibilities, it will have served the highest good. God blessed you, for you are loved.

*It's about time we start
to see it the earth is
our only home*

*It's about time we start
to face it we can't
make it here all alone*

*It's about time we start
to listen to the voices
in the wind*

*It's about time and it's
about changes and It's
about time.*

john denver

Resources

The following credits reflect those books and organizations that contributed to the creation of this book, in their influence on my thinking and awareness.

Lifespring: A human potentials course that puts many of the ideas and principles presented here into experiential context. Trainings are five-days intensives, in major cities. Central offices: 4340 Redwood Hwy., San Rafael, Ca. 94903.

Forum (EST): Similar to Lifespring. Also with offices in major cities.

Outward Bound: Classes in wilderness survival and adventure vacations. 384 Field Point Rd., Greenwich, CT 06830

I Come As A Brother: Mary Margaret Moore, channeling "Bartholomew". c/o High Mesa Press, P.O. Box 2267, Taos, NM 87571

Right Use Of Will: One World Publications, 110 Dartmouth SE, Albuquerque, NM 87106

Illusions: Richard Bach: Dell Publishing, any bookstore.

The Hundredth Monkey: Ken Keyes, Jr. Vision Books 790 Commercial Ave., Coos Bay, OR 97420

The Road Less Traveled: M. Scott Peck, Touchstone Books, any bookstore.

The Course in Miracles: A group discussion of contemporary Bible interpretation. Ask around. A metaphysical bookstore is a good place to start.

The Prophet: Kahlil Gilbran: Since 1923 a guide for many and a work of pure poetry. Alfred A. Knopf, Publisher. Any bookstore.

In Search Of Schrodinger's Cat: John Gribbin. A guide to quantum physics and reality. Bantam Books. Any bookstore.

Hanta Yo: Ruth Beebe Hill. Doubleday & Company, Warner Books Edition.

Loving Each Other: Leo F. Buscaglia. Fawcett Columbine. Any bookstore.

How to Meditate: Lawrence LeShan. A simple-to-understand straight forward look at the truth about meditation.

Creative Visualization: Shakti Gawain. Whatever Publishing Co. Mill Valley Calif.

Why men are the way they are: Warren Farrell, Ph.D. Must reading for every male.

Women who love too much: Robin Norwood: Must reading for every woman.

Way of the Peaceful Warrior: Dan Millman.

The Secrets Men Keep: Dr. Ken Druck, Ballantine Books, any bookstore.

The Power of Positive Thinking: Norman Vincent Peale, any bookstore.

The Americn Father: William Reynolds, Paddington Press.

Finding Our Fathers: Samual Osherson. The Free Press

Nurturing News: A quarterly newsletter for men about men. 187 Caselli Ave. San Francisco, Ca. 94114

Wingspan: Quarterly news of, by, and about the men's movement in America.

Life.

We at JOURNEYS TOGETHER publishing hope you have enjoyed reading this book. For ordering additional copies or further information on workshops, seminars and father and son wilderness adventures, please send this page to:

JOURNEYS TOGETHER PUBLISHING, P.O. Box 1254 La Mesa, CA 92044

Please send me the following:

_____copies of *Man in Transition* @ $9.95, postage paid.
(check enclosed for $............)

☐ Information on the *Father and Son Wilderness Adventures.*

☐ Information on *"The Man in Transition"* workshop.

Availability of *Ken Byers* for speaking to my group.

Other..

....

....

....

Name: .... Age: ...... Sex:...........

Address:..

City: .... State: .... Zip:....................

Ken Byers - January 1991

Aside from a full time career as a writer, Ken holds a degree in Engineering, is a practicing Industrial Designer, and business consultant, and is one of a handful of men currently studying for his Ph.D. in Men's Issues. He is a Certified Neuro-Linguistic Programming facilitator and professional speaker. As a member of the National Speakers Association, he speaks on men and women in relationships, and facilitates workshops for the general public and business groups in male/female communication. Additionally, he runs week long Father and Son Wilderness Relationship tours in the mountains of Arizona.

Mr. Byers has been associated with the Management Development Center at San Diego State University and has contributed articles to several national men's and business publications. As a nationally known voice for male advocacy, he is active in the promoting and setting up of men's issues groups across the country, and in personal consulting in San Diego.

Having successfully traveled the path of the traditional business world for twenty years, he retired in 1986 to write and to attempt to impact a meaningful integration of human potentials around the concept of improved human relationships, from the male perspective. His experience includes everything from successful entrepreneur to living penniless on the streets of San Diego. As a fatherless father of two boys himself, he has dedicated his life to the understanding of male growth through the father/son relationship, the father absent syndrome, and its powerful effect on the survival of our culture.